OLD FORGE

AF471270

AVRO ONE

by
Wg Cdr J. A. 'Robby' Robinson AFC, FrAeS, RAF (Retd)

Old Forge Publishing
England

Front Cover; Dramatic view of the ATP with the author in the left-hand seat during its first flight on the 6th August 1986.
Back Cover; A Nimrod MR.2 watches the sun go down. (Harry Holmes).

First Edition 2005

Published
by
Old Forge Publishing
39 Backgate
Cowbit
Lincolnshire
PE12 6AP
oldforgepub@aol.com
www.oldforgepublishing.org
01406 381313

ISBN 0-9544507-8-7

Printed for Old Forge Publishing
By

Biddles Ltd
24 Rollesby Road
Hardwick Industrial Estate
King's Lynn
Norfolk
PE30 4LS

01553 764728

Contents

Acknowledgements

"I dedicate this book to my dear wife Tricia, who supported me so loyally throughout my RAF career and the ups and downs of my time at Woodford. I wish that she were alive today to see this book finally published.

I would also like to dedicate it to my dear Bernadette who has encouraged me to take up my new career as an impoverished author.

There are far too many people to thank individually for their help in making my time at Woodford so enjoyable and giving me so much ammunition for this autobiography. However, I must thank three people for their help in producing this book; Sir Charles Masefield for writing such an excellent foreword and for his friendship, Harry Holmes for many of the photographs in the book and for his unfailing support at Woodford and last, but not least, Martyn Chorlton for taking a chance in publishing it."

Old Forge Publishing would also like to thank the following, for their help with supplying photography for 'Avro One'. Harry Holmes, Ian Lowe, Ray Sturtivant, Javier Ortega Figueiral and David Roura.

"Avro One" is the much coveted radio callsign, handed down from generation to generation, of successive Chief Test Pilots of the famous Avro Company based at Woodford, Cheshire - now, more prosaically, known as the Woodford Unit of BAE Systems.

Not only is this much prized and jealously guarded "Avro One" callsign of the Woodford Chief Test Pilot preserved to this day - surviving company name changes over the years from Avro through Hawker Siddeley and British Aerospace to BAE Systems – but also, uniquely in the history of aviation, the succession of "Avro" Chief Test Pilots stretches back unbroken for 97 years. Indeed it was on 8th June 1908 that Alliot Verdon Roe made the very first powered hops of a British aircraft in the UK – the Roe 1 Biplane. These hops took place along the finishing straight of the famous Brooklands race track. A.V.Roe subsequently undertook the first flights and testing of his next four designs – the Avro Triplane series – and in doing so unwittingly became the first in the long line of Avro Chief Test Pilots.

Alliot Verdon Roe the first of a long line of Avro Test Pilots and undoubtedly the first 'Avro One'.

By 1910, "AV" decided it was time that his mechanic Howard Pixton, learnt to fly. On 17th October 1910, Pixton attempted his very first take off – regrettably downwind – resulting in an ignominious early termination of the flight, nose first, into the famous Brooklands sewage farm. Undeterred and aircraft repaired, Pixton was airborne again on 8th November safely clearing the sewage farm but subsequently sideslipping into the ground whereupon the long suffering Roe IV Triplane caught fire. Nevertheless, the aircraft was again repaired and, with Pixton at the controls, was again in the air on 17th November and back into the sewage farm on 4th December! Despite these embarrassing and rather smelly early setbacks Pixton gained his airman's certificate on 24th January 1911 and, "AV" demonstrating supreme confidence in his new self taught test pilot, detailed him to make the first flight in March 1911 on his next design – the Avro Type D. Pixton went on to become one of the best known pre-war Test Pilots and a worthy early bearer of the Avro Chief Test Pilot title. Following Howard Pixton in this role came Wilfred Parke who, amongst other aircraft, made the first flight in 1912 of the world's first enclosed cockpit aircraft, the Avro Type F. Perhaps the best known, however, of the very early Avro Chief Test Pilots was Fred Raynham who made the first flight on the famous Avro 504 and occupied this demanding position throughout the First World War. Raynham was succeeded by H.A. Hamersley who was to hand over as Chief Test Pilot in the early 1920s to the legendary Australian from Bundaberg in

Queensland, Bert Hinkler. Hinkler tested all new Avro aircraft through the 1920s until, on 7th February 1928, he took off from Croydon in an Avro Avian on his famous record breaking solo flight. 15 and a half days later he landed at Darwin having covered 11,005 miles in a flying time of 128 hours. The record breaking Avian aircraft hangs from the roof of the Brisbane Museum to this day. Sadly, while still Chief Test Pilot, Bert Hinkler was to lose his life on another England to Australia record attempt when he crashed in the Alps in bad weather.

So started the long and distinguished tenure of the famous Captain H.A. (Sam) Brown as Avro Chief Test Pilot, lasting from the early 1930s until after the end of World War 2. Indeed, with the introduction of radios into aircraft, Sam Brown was the first to adopt the callsign "Avro One". Brown was to make the first flights of the Avro Manchester and it's derivative, perhaps the greatest wartime bomber ever built, the Avro Lancaster. Some 7,500 Lancasters were produced and several thousand of them left the ground for the first time in the hands of Sam Brown. His second in command throughout the war had been Bill Thorn who took over from the great man on his retirement. Sadly, Bill Thorn's period as Avro One was to be cut short when, on 23rd August 1947, he took off from Woodford in the Tudor 2, which had the aileron controls mistakenly crossed during installation thereby operating in the reverse sense. Chief Designer Roy Chadwick was also on board and, when the aircraft rolled into the ground from 50 feet altitude, tragically both he and Bill Thorn were killed.

Robby Robinson (left), Sir Charles Masefield (Centre) and Jimmy Orrell, three ex Chief Test Pilots who held the title of 'Avro One'. An example of another Avro success story rests in the background; the Shackleton.

Long time Avro Test Pilot Jimmy Orrell, who had also tested more than 1,000 Lancasters during the war, became the third to inherit the Avro One callsign. On 6th September 1948 Jimmy was to achieve fame as the first man in the world to fly a four engined jet airliner – the RR Nene engined Tudor 8 – which took to the air from Woodford nearly a year before the first flight of the DH Comet. Jimmy also became the first man to fly a jet airliner in North America when, on 10th August 1949 at Malton, Ontario, he made the first flight of the Avro Canada C-102 Jetliner.

With the advent of the revolutionary Vulcan programme, Wing Commander Roly Falk, who had previously tested the little Avro 707 – mini Vulcan – experimental Delta at Boscombe Down, was brought in to fly the futuristic V bomber. In the summer of 1952, Falk duly took the Vulcan into the air for the first time. A few days later, having rapidly accumulated 10 hours flying time, Falk took the Vulcan to the Farnborough Air Show and astonished the aviation community by rolling it during his display. Falk's brilliant and high profile flying of the Vulcan did much to secure Government confidence to order the type in quantity, but it was not until Jimmy Harrison became "Avro One" that the true development and refinement of the aircraft's handling characteristics and performance took place. Jimmy went on to undertake development flying of Avro's next aircraft – the highly successful 748 short haul Turboprop airliner. Much of the 748's worldwide sales success for the next 25 years around the world was due to it's outstanding short field capability. Indeed, so spectacularly short had been Jim's measured short landing for certification, that for all the developments and derivatives of the aircraft over the subsequent years these landing distances were merely extrapolated – none of us who followed Jim dared to repeat this certification test, convinced that we could never match, let alone beat, his brilliant performance.

Following Jim Harrison as Avro One came Tony Blackman, my first boss, and it was a test education to fly with him. Tony was widely known to be without equal for the vast number of "test points" he could complete on any given flight. When airborne, one's head spun trying to keep up with him. Indeed I recall that when I first started flying with him in Victor or Vulcan aircraft my main preoccupation was to try to complete the time consuming process of strapping into the ejection seat and all the pre-take off checks before we were actually roaring down the runway. I must have passed muster because when Tony retired I had the good fortune and privilege to be selected to succeed him as "Avro One" leading on to the enjoyment of undertaking the first flight and early development of the strangely shaped AEW Nimrod.

My great good fortune as Chief Test Pilot was to have Robby Robinson as my deputy and subsequent successor as "Avro One". Never can there have been anyone better qualified for such a role. Robby had been a V bomber pilot in the Royal Air Force and a graduate of the Empire Test Pilots School where subsequently he became a tutor and, as a Wing Commander, he returned as the ETPS boss and Chief Instructor. What a pleasure he was to work with and to fly with. Whether on the ground or in the air he was always relaxed, unflustered and full of humour and ready to see the funny side of any situation. He also had that unmistakable quality of exceptional pilots – soft hands. I well remember undertaking his Nimrod refresher trip shortly after his arrival at Woodford.

No sooner had we selected wheels and flaps up after take off and become established in the climb, than I asked the crew if anyone could smell burning? Negative answers came back from throughout the aircraft so I turned to Robby and asked "Can't you smell it?" With one hand on the controls, he used the other to remove a large, heavily smoking cigar, from his mouth with the contented reply "Can't smell a thing".

  Who better to tell the story of Avro One in the 1980s than Robby Robinson. Here is an insight into the varied life as a company test pilot of that time told by a true professional with the interest, clarity and humour which are his hallmark. You will thoroughly enjoy this read.

Robby Robinson and Jimmy Orrell are joined by Jimmy Harrison (right). Harrison was instrumental in refining the handling qualities of the Avro Vulcan and also helped make the HS.748 a best seller for Hawker Siddeley for almost 25 years.

Avro One

Chapter One

Becoming Civilised

"Okay, you're on." So saying, Tony Blackman, Hawker Siddeley's Chief Test Pilot at Woodford, moved away to chat to a group of fellow guests. This ended a rather unusual job interview. The occasion was the 1977 Battle of Britain cocktail party at Boscombe Down. I, as the Chief Instructor of the Empire Test Pilots School, was one of the hosts and my wife Tricia and I were having a lovely time yelling at old friends in the large anteroom of the Officer's Mess. Every year the party gets bigger and noisier and I was having my usual high tone deafness difficulties trying to hear what the ladies were saying. By the look of the small blonde opposite me I had probably laughed when she told me that her mother had died last week. However, I heard Tony when he sidled up beside me with his wife Margaret.

"Robby, I need another test pilot. Can you think of anyone available?" he shouted. As the boss of ETPS I was used to being used as an employment agency and I went into a well-rehearsed resume of those tp's that I knew were leaving the service soon. Tony turned them all down.

"Well Tony," I said eventually, "It depends on how much you are willing to pay. If it's enough someone might be willing to leave the RAF early."

"Ten thousand" he said unblinkingly. To an impoverished Wing Commander that seemed a fortune in 1977.

"For that," I said slowly, "I'll come myself."

"Okay, you're on." He said and moved away, pulling Margaret with him.

"Call me."

My first move was to seek out Tricia and tell her about it. After the party and over the weekend we talked of little else. It was a big decision, I had had no intention of leaving the air force; it was my life.

I was born in Gloucester in 1932 and we lived in Longleavens, a village near the big RAF camp at Innsworth and near Staverton airfield. My father worked for the Gloster Aircraft Company and my great uncle was the Chief Engine Designer at the Bristol Aircraft Company. So, even before the war, I had an interest in flying and when it started there was no holding me. Our house was always full of airmen of many nationalities, as was the WVS canteen run by my mother, where I learnt to speak a few words of Polish and cadge chewing gum from the Canadians and then the Americans. A few school friends and I formed an aeromodelling and aircraft recognition club in Porky Holmes' kitchen. (We could tell the mark of a Spitfire by the sound of it's engine). Like every boy of that age, I was aeroplane mad so as soon as I could I joined the Air Training Corps at my school, Sir Thomas Rich's. When the war ended my interest did not abate and a visit to the school of an RAF recruiting officer made me aware of the Royal Air Force College Cranwell. I applied and went for the medical and aptitude tests towards the end of 1949. To the surprise of my headmaster, I passed and started there as a Cadet in April 1950. I am thus one of a dying breed who swore allegiance to a King.

I spent three hard years at Cranwell that seemed like purgatory at the time but, unlike some others, I did not have the moral fibre to resign. So I managed to last out, even becoming a Flight Cadet Under Officer in my final term. After graduation in December 1952, I did my jet training on Meteors and then flew Canberras on 10 Squadron and Valiants on 90 Squadron until in 1961 managed to pass the entrance examinations for ETPS.

The next year, 1962, changed my life completely. Mind you, I was still the brash party boy of yore, if not more so, but now aeroplanes became the centre of my life. They were no longer work tools that some genius had designed and presented me with, but things to understand and assess. At last I was the bad workman who was not only expected to blame his tools but paid to do so. I had entered a very exclusive brotherhood that crossed not only service lines but also the service/civil divide and international borders. In 1988, the BBC made an excellent series of programmes about ETPS that showed how hard the students have to work and went some way towards explaining the motivation that makes this possible. I cannot say that I had a driving ambition towards being a test pilot, but that was because it had always seemed quite out of my reach. Test pilots were gods and Chief Test Pilots super gods. It was only when Jock Cochrane, a fellow captain on 90 Squadron, passed for the school that I realised that I too could perhaps do it.

ETPS was in those days situated at Farnborough and I would have been quite happy to stay there after graduation. However, the powers that be thought otherwise. They promoted me and posted me to B Squadron at the Aeroplane and Armament Experimental Establishment, which is quite a mouthful. Even it's more usually used initials, A&AEE, scarcely slip easily off the tongue, so I will from now on just use it's location, Boscombe Down. The airfield is situated on the southern edge of Salisbury Plain and is often subject to bleak winter weather. Early 1963 was such a time and I, and others posted there, were unable to fight our way through the deep snow on the Andover to Amesbury road for two weeks. But eventually the snow melted somewhat and, leaving Tricia and our children, Keri and Simon, in our married quarter at Farnborough, I set out in my faithful old Ford V8 Pilot loaded down with my flying kit and most of my worldly goods. The journey was memorable because it took two days, largely due to the car shedding both water pumps, as it was prone to do, and losing all it's anti-freeze. A night spent in a transport cafe was a fitting way to deflate the ego of a new and very green Squadron Leader. So, when I eventually rolled into the Mess car park at dinnertime I was suitably chastened and ready to be impressed by even a modest standard of messing. To walk into the dining room and to be warmly welcomed by a dozen or so residents tucking in to pheasant from the airfield shoot and drinking a good claret was beyond my imagining. Many years later I became President of the Mess Committee and I like to think that I maintained the same standards. My figure and arteries bear this out.

I stayed at Boscombe Down for three years, one on B Squadron which was responsible for the acceptance of all large aircraft, and the last two as the Senior Pilot on the newly formed E Squadron, a new squadron that was split away from B to deal with the large number of new transport aircraft coming into service. All in all I had a great time. I flew everything that I could get my hands on. In particular, the Victor, Belfast, 748, Argosy and Beverley. I grew to like really big aeroplanes whilst still being able to indulge my sense of excitement in the small jets such as the Hunter and the Meteor. I dropped torpedoes from Shackletons, heavy loads from Beverleys, Argosys and 748s and snatched loads out of the Beverley using an arrester wire on the ground and a hook on the back end of the aircraft. I was able to share in the company testing of several aircraft and got to know the test pilots at Belfast and Woodford very well whilst previewing the Belfast aircraft and the Queens Flight 748. A really exciting three years.

Six Hawker Siddeley Andover CC.2s were delivered to RAF between July 1964 and September 1965, including XS790 seen here undergoing trials with the A&AEE. Only the nose survives today, ironically at the Boscombe Down Museum. (via RCS).

I was very sorry to leave Boscombe at the end of 1965 when I was posted to the RAF Staff College, Bracknell. My sadness being compounded by being on the ground for the first time in sixteen years. I remember remarking to a fellow student on the course, who was made of sterner stuff, that I felt like an athlete out of training. He replied that that was a rather immature point of view. He went on to become an Air Marshal before he retired, but I kept flying until I was 67 and I think that I did better than he.

I received the news of my posting at the end of Staff College with a heavy heart. It was slightly lightened by the fact that it was to be in Intelligence, but it was to be a three-year ground tour. Strangely enough I quite enjoyed the challenge of the job and was able to use my test flying experience to good advantage. However, I was overjoyed when, after only nine months, I was told that I had been asked for as a tutor at ETPS. The school was about to move from Farnborough to Boscombe Down so I uprooted my family yet again and moved out of our small house in South London to yet another married quarter at our old stamping ground. Tricia and the children were as pleased as I was, even though it was our eleventh move in fourteen years of marriage.

The word tutor suggests an academic post, ground based. However, at ETPS the tutors are very definitely on a flying tour. They not only teach the esoteric art of report writing but also convert their students to the various types of aircraft, teach them test techniques and, above all, they carry out the balancing act of training the students to assess. This is similar to teaching someone to become a wine taster. There are no correct answers, only good opinions. I may one day write about my time at ETPS so I will save my ammunition until then, but I did enjoy my three years as a tutor and it taught me a lot about human behaviour.

I left ETPS at the end of 1970 on another posting to MOD. This time to Air Plans, which is the policy branch of the Air Staff. My feeling of depression on this latest grounding was partially offset by my being promoted to Wing Commander and I again surprised myself by quite enjoying the job. Nevertheless, the commuting from our Farnborough married quarter every day was a real drag and the news that I was to go back to Boscombe as the Deputy Superintendent of Flying arrived just in time to prevent me going into a terminal decline.

For the next two years I served as Group Captain John Wilkinson's deputy. I knew him well from my time at Cranwell, he being in 56 Entry and me in 57. John is inclined to be a little eccentric at times but then so am I, so we got on fine. The Deputy S of F post is no job for the young, thrusting, upwardly mobile Wing Commander but for two years it suited me fine. I needed a rest after three hectic years in the cut and thrust of MOD and the job specification was just right. I flew once or twice a week in Hunters or Canberras or anything else I could bluff my way into. In particular, I was able to renew my affair with an early love, the Harvard, and carry out photo-chases to record heavy drops. There is something truly magical about tucking in very close to the wing tip of a large aircraft and then banking hard to spiral down round the load, filming the opening of it's parachutes. I always signed off with a bit of legal hooliganism at ultra low level over Salisbury Plain. Then home for tea. One of my unofficial duties was to tend the pheasants being reared on the airfield in preparation for the winter shoots. I also did a stint as the President of the Mess Committee and, as I indicated earlier, this secondary duty mixed well with the Station shoot. The only negative aspect of the job was that I was a sitting duck when it came to choosing someone to be the President of any Court Martial in the Command. I did not enjoy that position of power.

Two years as Deputy S of F was a great rest cure but I began to champ at the bit and wanted to get back to more productive work. Fate took a hand when the powers that be decided that the Commanding Officer of ETPS should cease to be a Group Captain's post and that the school should no longer be autonomous but should come under the S of F and the Head of the school would be a Wing Commander with the title of Chief

Instructor. I volunteered immediately and slid gratefully into the seat in January 1976. Group Captain Mike Adams, who had been the CO of ETPS, became the S of F so the transition was pretty smooth, with a minimum change of cast.

So began my final RAF tour, although I did not know it. The Chief Instructor assumed the duties of the old CO but with the distinct advantage of being an active member of the flying staff. So my two years as CI passed pleasurably and all too quickly. At the end of 1977 I was contacted by the Air Secretary's branch that looks after the fate of all RAF officers and was told that all the whining in the world would not prevent me being grounded again. I'd had it too good, they said, and would be attending the Air Warfare course at Cranwell in the New Year. This could lead to promotion I knew, but this did not make up for the fact that my grounding could be forever. I was by now 45 years old and very unlikely to get another flying tour, especially if I was promoted. Tony Blackman's approach at the cocktail party could therefore not have come at a better time. Although I talked it over with Tricia for two days, we both knew that the decision had been taken at the party.

The pace of the school year hotted up as the final term came to an end. I was as usual frantically busy with final assessments and postings and the all-important allocation of awards to the graduating students. It was difficult in the rush to come to terms with the fact that my 28 years in the RAF were coming to an end, but I realized that part of my motivation to leave came from the need to prove myself outside the comfortable cocoon of the service. My first move was to resign from the RAF and that was a difficult letter to write. In parallel with my letter Tony also wrote to the Air Secretary. The reaction to his letter was that I was the most valuable officer that had ever graced the service, (I wished that they had told me that before), and that they would, under no circumstances, countenance my leaving for at least another 3 years. It was a predictable reaction as quite a number of middle rank officers were leaving at the time. However, they gave in gracefully (and, I thought, with indecent haste) after Hawker Siddley brought in their big guns and letters were exchanged at Air Staff level. So suddenly I was out of the Air Force and, more importantly, soon to be out of my married quarter with no house to go to. We had never owned a house and to buy one for the first time and at long range was daunting. I also needed to get a civil license, so time for thought and regret was limited.

Because of the house hunting, I elected to go for a home study course to prepare for the CAA

Despite having flown for many hours in the RAF's Andovers, the CAA would not allow Robby to fly the civil registered HS.748.

examinations for my ATPL civil license. I wrote to Avigation, a company situated in Ealing. On receiving the course notes I was surprised that my 28 years of flying counted for nothing. It was fair enough for me to be examined in Air Law and navigation but to have to take exams in basic subjects such as electrics and magnetism and Morse code, all of which I had studied at Cranwell, seemed to be an enormous waste of human time and endeavour. Of course I failed, but by this time I had arrived at Woodford and was flying RAF registered aircraft such as the Comet 4c with the big AEW radar nose and the Nimrod Mk 2 undergoing development. I had been flying the 748 in the service for many years but the CAA would not let me fly the civil registered 748 without passing their examination. I still think the whole system needs a rethink.

I arrived at Woodford in April 1978 and moved into an office in the Flight Operations department. It was not a pretty "site". It faced the supersonic wind tunnel and our days were punctuated by a klaxon horn which warned that a high speed, very noisy run was about to take place. I noted that in the gents' toilet downstairs was a notice stating that ear defenders must be donned when the horn sounded. I cannot remember anyone taking such items to the toilet - even putting fingers in one's ears whilst in a critical position courted disaster! I shared the office with John Stockwell, a navigator who had left the RAF a few months earlier. On the first morning John asked me how my exams were going. "Fine." I said, "I'm waiting for my results and I take my performance exam at Manchester Airport tomorrow, Wednesday." John looked at me strangely. "Today *is* Wednesday." He said. I ran from the building to my car and drove the six miles in record time. By the time I had found the examination room, I was 45 minutes late for an exam that lasted an hour and a half and I had missed my final night of swotting. Maybe I should have taken all the exams this way, because this one I passed.

Tony Blackman had left by this time to go as a Director of Smiths Industries and Charles Masefield, son of Sir Peter, had taken over as Chief Test Pilot. Charles was very sympathetic to my exam problem and suggested that I take a quick revision course before re-sitting; the Company would pay, which was very generous. So I found myself in Ealing for two weeks, enrolled at Avigation, which occupied offices above some shops in Ealing Broadway. Every day, with a dozen or so other hopefuls, I sat at a small table, facing the Broadway, working through specimen exam papers over and over again. The school was run by a Mr. Nabarro, the brother of Gerald Nabarro the well-known MP, and he looked very like him, even to the handlebar moustache. It was rather weird to be lectured by a man who apparently appeared in the newspapers almost daily. Mr. Nabarro was a heavy smoker and the classroom was covered in a fine silt of cigarette ash. You always knew when he was looking over your shoulder because invariably a large splodge of ash would fall on your answer sheet. At the end of the two weeks we congregated in London University to re-sit our various exams. To Mr. Nabarro's everlasting credit we all passed.

At some time during this period, I took my civil instrument rating at Manchester. Another hurdle to overcome. It took a month of flying to come up to standard as neither my instructor nor I could fly every day. I was busy testing Nimrods and Bob Abbot, the instructor, was busy on his primary job as a Captain with Britannia Airways. He was a very good instructor if sometimes a little "different". One day, as I sat waiting in the Manchester school of flying, he burst in and declared that he could not fly today as he had to go home to look after his wife: some ducks had flown into their bedroom and one had drowned itself in the water jug. I never did work that one out. It was the end of June before the CAA's Captain Dai Reese, in a fit of generosity, passed me. He signed my IRT form on the 28th and on the 29th I flew down to Dunsfold in the Company Dove and got a lift to the CAA's headquarters in London. I entered clutching all my various certificates to claim my much-prized license. The spotty youth in pullover and trainers behind the desk took my paperwork and a cheque for a large amount of money and disappeared. I sat down to wait. He returned after some time with a mug of tea in his hand and, looking at me he said:

"Yes?"

"I'm waiting for my license."

"It'll take a week."

"What, just for a signature?"

"That's right." He said turning away.

"Just a minute." I exploded, rising to my feet to demonstrate that I had six inches, three stone and twenty-five years on him. "I have to fly to Trinidad on Monday and I need my license for a job I have to do out there."

He remained unimpressed but his boss, a Mr. Phillips, whose signature I required, heard the rumpus and, recognizing a trouble maker when he heard one, came out of his office, took my paperwork with him and reappeared one minute later to hand me my signed license. I learned a sound lesson from this. When dealing with minor functionaries, create a fuss, go over their heads. You always find that the higher you go the more helpful they are.

I was now ready to face the civil world. Charles decided that I should not be allowed to catch my breath and pushed me in at the deep end. TTAS (The Trinidad and Tobago Air Services), had bought three new 748s, their registration numbers being 9Y-TFS, 9Y-TFT and 9Y-TFX. TTAS immediately christened them Too F***ing Small, Too F***ing Tiny and Too F***ing Expensive, which we were to deliver. On the 5th of July, Tony Hawks and I, together with Steve Fawley, the engineer, set off across the Atlantic, the first of many times I was to make this journey in a 748. I see from my logbook that we made it from Woodford to Keflavik in Iceland, to Narssarssuak in Greenland and to Sept Isles in Canada in one day, a very long haul. We were obviously making the best of the long summer days in those high latitudes. The leg to Narssarssuak was memorable for the last thirty miles. The airfield lies on the western coast of Greenland at the foot of a glacier and at the end of a long fiord that winds between granite walls rising several thousand feet. We began by letting down to sea level and heading for a radio beacon at the mouth of the fiord. We then set out along the inlet, hoping that we had chosen the right one. The cloud base was below the tops of the surrounding walls and we flew low over broken ice floes until we reached a beached and very rusty freighter on the north shore. We noted this with relief, as it was the only landmark in the fiord that was marked on the map and showed that we were on the right track. If we had chosen wrongly we would have had to find a widening of the channel that would allow us enough room to turn around and fly back out to sea. We now pressed on with enough confidence to enjoy the view. The airfield eventually appeared at the end of the fiord, not exactly an international airport but it looked good to us. After clearance by an Inuit customs officer, and having duly paid our landing fees, we refuelled and set off in the reverse direction. We flew as close to the right hand cliffs as we dared, mindful of the possibility of someone else flying towards us. The hotel at Sept Isles was a welcome respite.

Early next morning we set off for Nassau, calling in at Greensboro to refuel, and booked into a Trust House Forte hotel that seemed rather out of place in the tropics. I remember that we sat down to dinner feeling somewhat punch drunk and remarking that it looked as though a tropical storm was approaching. The storm duly arrived with much thunder and lightning and with the sound of heavy rain. This soon passed but fifteen minutes later it happened again. By this time a few gin and tonics and a bottle of wine had disappeared and it took several repeats of the storm for us to realize that they all sounded exactly alike and that between them tropical birds twittered, at eleven o'clock at night! Our suspicions were confirmed when we staggered out of the restaurant to find a beautiful, clear, tropical, moonlit night outside. I have often tried to go back to the restaurant but have never been able to find it with it's artificial microclimate. Our last leg, the next day, took us to St Croix, where a large, pistol toting US customs man presented each of us with a small bottle of rum, and finally to Piarco airport, Trinidad.

Tony and Steve immediately caught a plane home, not even staying one night, because we were short handed back at base. I found my way to the Hilton in the dark and booked into this very luxurious hotel. It took me a little time to find my room, or even my floor. Every time I pressed the button for the sixteenth floor the lift went down. After several excursions back to the reception desk the truth hit home. The hotel was built upside down. Reception was at the top of the building and the other floors were spread down the front of a cliff overlooking the city of Port of Spain.

I was in the middle of a much needed shower, feeling rather lonely in this strange land, when the phone rang. It was Ken Pinder, a pilot flying for TTAS on a short contract. He invited me to meet him in the bar downstairs, (sorry, upstairs) and I needed no urging to

One of the three HS.748s belonging to TTAS pictured at Crown Point airport in Tobago. The tractor was in the same livery as the aircraft!

take up his kind offer. I hastily dressed and, this time with no difficulty, I unerringly homed in on the bar. Ken was a very entertaining chap, very practised in leading others astray. In me he had a willing victim. I had been given a voucher for a free drink when I booked in and I now redeemed it for a large Coco Loco; a delicious, "innocuous" fruit drink served in a mock coconut shell and sipped through a straw. It seemed so nice that I had several more. We had a jolly night and I went to bed feeling no pain. The next morning was different, I met Ken at breakfast who was obviously used to this sort of thing and was noisily tucking into bacon and eggs and, at the same time, smoking his first cigarette of the day. I was not feeling well.

HS.748   9Y-TFS unloading at Piarco International airport in Tobago.

My first duty was to visit the local Department of Civil Aviation to have my license validated for use in Trinidad. When I eventually found the office, which was situated in a large old house, I thought that they were recovering from a rather bad fire. The walls were blackened and the filing cabinets bulging with papers that spilled out over leprous linoleum. The desks appeared to be charred and the chairs looked as though the fire brigade had been at them with axes. I was later to find that the offices always looked like that, and had done so for as long as anyone could remember. Perhaps they moved in after the previous owners had been burnt out. Eventually I was warmly greeted by an Indian gentleman who I got to know quite well in the following years.

"Welcome Captain," he said.

This filled me with a glow of satisfaction; he was the first person to ever call me Captain. He took my pristine license, glanced at the photograph in it and then announced that he would have to ask me some questions on Trinidadian Air law. I went cold, nobody had warned me of this. I was not ready for another examination and I would fail and be sent ignominiously back to the UK.

"Which wing is the red light on?" he said.

"Pardon!" I replied, mystified.

He repeated the question.

"It's on the port wing." I said hopefully.

"Okay, you've passed." He said with a smile, stamping my license.

That afternoon, Mike Nobriga, the TTAS Chief Pilot, flew with me on two sectors, to

Crown Point airport in Tobago and back. He then cleared me to fly the line for them. I flew this route for the next week, Piarco to Crown Point and back up to four times a day or night. By the end of your duty you found it hard to remember how many times you had flown these sectors. It took only twenty minutes from off chocks at Piarco to on chocks at Crown Point.

Final approach into Crown Point, Tobago with Robby at the controls of HS.748 9Y-TFS.

The flight consisted of a quick left turn after take off, climbing to 2,000 feet over the hills to the north, cruise for 2 to 3 minutes and then a gentle descent onto a right base approach to the picturesque runway rising from the sea at Crown Point. The hardest parts were avoiding the pelicans diving for fish off the near end of the runway, and having to squeeze off the runway onto the pan in front of the tiny terminal building. This semi-circular pan only held three aircraft but often four of us were squashed in and sometimes a fifth aircraft was left waiting on the runway until the first in the queue taxied out. One night the pilot of a DC-9 jet on finals asked me if my tail was clear of the runway. "I don't know." I replied, "You're closer than I am." On one occasion I parked the aircraft as close as I dared behind a DC-9 and went into the terminal to check the passenger manifest. I heard the jet start up and looked out of the window. The pilot of the DC-9, for some reason, used a lot of power to get moving. I ran out as I saw our props whirling round in the jet blast, just in time to see the rear passenger door blown inside out, breaking the stays. I ruefully examined the damage and concluded that with a bit of work on the door we could fly back unpressurised. For safety's sake we would carry no passengers.

We had no tools on the aircraft so I walked over to the fire station and borrowed some from the Chief Fire Officer's car boot. However, I found that Ford Cortina spanners did not fit Hawker Siddley aircraft and I was reduced to removing the remains of the stays with my trusty Swiss Army penknife. We eventually managed to take off the whole door and, whilst we two pilots and one hostess offered it up to the frame, the other hostess managed to lock it from the inside. It's all in a day's work to an airline pilot.

Before I had flown out to Trinidad I had received a call from Peter Sedgewick, a Falkland Islander who had been Senior Tutor at ETPS when I was the boss. He was leaving the RAF to join an airline and was entitled to a resettlement course. "Could you do anything for me?" I knew that Woodford was having difficulties in finding pilots to support TTAS so I suggested to Charles Masefield that Peter could go to Trinidad for his months "course". Charles jumped at the idea and, after I had left for the Caribbean, Peter had been given a quick check out on the 748 to get it on his civil license. So, one night, after I had arrived back at the Hilton, I wandered down to the swimming pool where the Prime Minister, of all people, was hosting a television programme on drumming, or "drumology" as he called it. And there was Peter, sitting in the spotlights as part of the background audience. I joined him and raised my glass as I greeted him.

"Cheers Peter. Funny old world isn't it?"

Peter's wife Hilary joined him later and I believe that the prize for the most outrageous resettlement course must go to him as, not only did he do it from the Hilton Hotel Port of Spain, but got paid for it as well.

The next day I checked him out on the route and then checked in at the airport for my flight home that evening. I had no time to change, merely to take off my Captain's bars. I was reluctant to give up my first taste of luxury living in the tropics and queued up on the tarmac for my seat on the British Airways 747 with many regrets. It was a lovely evening with the stars coming out and the airfield lights twinkling. I was just congratulating myself on having completed my first civil assignment successfully when 9Y-TFX, the aircraft I had delivered just a week ago, screeched to a halt in front of me on the taxiway. The rear door opened and a large athletic looking gentleman leapt out and ran off across the airfield. I was nonplussed, but decided that I had a certain responsibility as the nearest representative of the aircraft's builder. So I tentatively left the queue and walked towards the 748. As I did so the one engine that was still turning stopped and the rest of the passengers swarmed out of the overwing emergency exits and the two pilots, Ken Pinder and Peter Sedgewick, left by the front door. We met halfway and they told me their story as the fire vehicles arrived with bells and blue lights going, and the ex-passengers ran around in panic.

Apparently an engine fire warning light had illuminated just after take off and Ken had very sensibly stopped the engine and turned back for an emergency landing. As they cleared the runway the hostess had done her duty perfectly. She had picked the largest, fittest passenger she could see and had asked him to climb out of the door, down the escape rope, and to steady the bottom of the escape chute for the other passengers to slide down. This was the man I had seen disappearing into the night. I commiserated with the two pilots, especially as the fire warning had been spurious, but I felt that I could do little to help, and anyway the ground crew round the 747 were preparing to pull the steps away.

"Have a nice time Pete." I flung over my shoulder. "See you back home." I ran for my aircraft. I did not see Peter for two years. I sank into my business class seat and accepted a large, cool gin and tonic. I felt well and truly civilised.

overleaf: TTAS HS.748 9Y-TFX over Crown Point airport in Tobago.

TTAS Trinida
MICHAEL CIPRIANI

go Air Services
9Y-TFX

Chapter Two

Flying the Line

Something that I had never realised from the safety of the RAF was that civil test pilots do not spend all their time testing aircraft. Besides the fact that there is a lot of paper-work and meetings to attend, there is not enough actual testing to occupy all the pilots all the time. Test work comes in peaks and troughs. For long periods there is almost no test flying and then suddenly there is so much that there are not enough pilots to cope. Luckily the troughs can be filled by a variety of other sorts of flying. Aircraft companies also employ training pilots, demonstration pilots etc. The tp's on the payroll help out at all these tasks: they are the perfect multi-purpose weapon. We are very happy to fill in at these other roles and the feedback of customer requirements improves the product. I certainly had my fill of other sorts of flying during my time at Woodford. When an air-craft has been successfully sold to an airline, the first task is to train their crews and to introduce the aircraft onto the airline's routes. This requires a certain amount of self-confidence, not to say cockiness, especially when you have never done it before. Ignorance is bliss, and there must be several airlines in the more backward parts of the world that still use the Robinson system of selling tickets, loading freight and flight planning. Linhas Aereas Da Guiné-Bissau is not truly such an airline, but that is because it uses the José Pombo method.

I first met in José 1978 when he was introduced to me by Charles Masefield. I had been at Woodford for just six months and Charles in his usual kindly manner decided to push me in at the deep end, again.

"Robby" he said, in his office one morning, "This is Captain Pombo. He is Chief Pilot of Guiné-Bissau Airlines and I have just explained that I have specially selected you to go out there with him to train his crews and to fly the line for a bit to introduce the aircraft."

I shook hands with the small, dark Portuguese man before me and we immediately fell to discussing how I would approach the task. I had to conceal several facts during these discussions, such as that I had, as yet, never trained anyone on the 748, that my only experience of flying the line was my one week in Trinidad, and that I had no idea where the hell Guiné-Bissau was. I also did not reveal that this was the first time that I had heard of this task. I still reckon that Charles looked out of his window and I happened to be the first pilot to pass. However, I liked the look of José and he obviously knew all there was to know about flying in Africa. (For I found that Guiné-Bissau was indeed in Africa, just above the armpit). He had been in the country when it was owned by Portugal, and had actually fought in the Portuguese Airforce there during the war of independence. After Portugal suddenly relinquished it's hold on all it's colonies in the mid-seventies he had been asked by the Marxist President to stay on and run all the aviation interests in the country; a pretty unique honour I would think. He was a first class pilot and a very engaging companion. I was going to enjoy this, I thought.

Our first task was to fly the aircraft (they had only bought one) so that José could check that it met their specifications. He soon showed that he was no fool and we had to fly it again the next day after several things had been put right before he would sign for G-BFVR, as it was temporarily registered. He disappeared after a quick training flight on the 12th October. I believe that he went to Lisbon to arrange finance. Guiné-Bissau, at that time, was a very poor country and had no credit in any country so José had to carry vast amounts of currency to pay all the bills. The aircraft was provided under an aid agreement involving Portugal in some way, hence José's visit and our short stay there a few weeks later. He did not re-appear until the end of November for the remainder of his training. I really had no need to teach him anything, I merely made a few suggestions as he found out about the aircraft for himself, so the training period was short and we were ready to go on the first of December. Would I be home in time for Christmas? A perennial question at Woodford.

Our party consisted of José and me, Jack Howard and Tom Cordener, customer support engineers, and Brian Jackson the ground school instructor. The aircraft was loaded with luggage and spares, including a spare Dart engine, and quite a bit of loot José had bought for Christmas presents. There was very little room for the non-pilots to sit at the back. We set off in the afternoon for the relatively short leg to Lisbon where I expected to stay for just one night. I had not reckoned with Portuguese bureaucracy.

We booked into the Lisbon Penta hotel for the night and decided to go out on the town. José was treating us and we were to dine at a famous fish restaurant in the city centre. At eight o'clock prompt two taxis arrived driven by unshaven bandits; José and Brian set off in the first and Tom, Jack and I climbed into the second. Our driver spoke not a word of English and my Portuguese was limited to ordering a glass of beer, learnt at the bar as we waited. He soon made his opinion of the first driver's navigation clear however, and with an Iberian shrug and an oath, he swung violently into a side road to avoid, we presumed, the city centre. Unknown to us, (and, it transpired, to the taxi driver), the day was the glorious 1st of December, or something, when the Portuguese celebrate their liberation. The police expected trouble and had isolated the centre of the city, including our restaurant, from all vehicular traffic. The first taxi had just made it before the ban came into force but we, due to our short cut, missed it by some minutes. I learnt all this from a traffic policeman who held a violent conversation with our driver at a barrier. Eventually, we swung round in the street, mounting the opposite pavement, and tore off to try some other avenue of access. None were available and we found ourselves getting deeper into the dark, menacing back streets.

As we could get no explanation from the driver we began to feel uneasy and, when he pulled into a blind alley, got out of the car and vehemently signalled for us to get out, we became distinctly panicky. As I attempted to remonstrate with him our small, shifty chauffeur set off up the hilly street and beckoned for us to follow him. We wound our way round back alleys and courtyards for about fifteen minutes until suddenly we came out opposite a large plate glass window behind which José and Brian grinned over their beers. I cannot imagine a London taxi driver completing his contract of delivery on foot, but full marks to Ernesto who showed a singular determination to earn his tip. With a sweeping gesture, and the Portuguese equivalent of "voila" he ushered us in and, at our invitation, joined us in a beer, then oysters, lobster, monkfish, dessert, coffee, liquors and cigars. After several hours of good companionship we persuaded him that we would be better off ordering a fresh taxi and that we would drop him off at home. He could collect his taxi tomorrow.

The next day José left to negotiate with some bankers whilst I set about the simple task of submitting our flight plan for the next leg and paying our handling fees. At that time the Portuguese government was trying to solve the unemployment problem by making it illegal to sack anyone. After some months this had the effect of doubling up the number of government employees doing any one job. Every desk in the airport offices had two people behind it, one to serve and the other to check. Not only was this time consuming but they had avoided the only merit in the system by refusing to run shifts and both men and women at every position went to lunch at the same time. I was given the usual run around of not being able to file my flight plan until I had paid my landing fees, and not being able to pay my fees until my flight plan had been signed. This is a common game around the world but the Portuguese had refined it to a degree only surpassed by the Indians. In the middle of my negotiations they all stood up and went to lunch. Finally, I gave up and decided that we were not going to leave today, so we went back to the hotel. As it happened, José did not appear for two days until, on the night of the third of December he met me in the bar with a big grin on his face. His negotiations had been successful and we could proceed. We left Lisbon in the afternoon of the next day, stayed the night in Las Palmas and then on to Bissau City, arriving there in the late afternoon.

This was my first taste of tropical Africa and it was colourful. The airfield was just one moderately long paved runway with several hangars off to one side and surrounded by creeks and inlets and mangrove swamps. The first thing we noticed was the jumbo sized mosquitoes that sized us up and chose Jack Howard as the sweetest meat. We decided to leave the unloading until the next day and piled aboard a rickety minibus for the ride to the hotel. The road to town was quite impressive, a dual carriageway in good repair. We found out later that it had been built by Sweden as part of it's aid and was the only paved road in the country. Even this ended in the square in front of the President's palace. The standard of housing along the road was distinctly variable, being composed of decaying huts on the outskirts of the town but in the town itself we passed rows of bungalows that would not have looked out of place in Surbiton, but even those were unpainted and tatty. There was a football stadium and several bars but only one or two shops and they had no goods in their windows. Things were obviously at a low ebb in Bissau City and the hotel, The Grand, was well up to standard.

The hotel was situated in a leafy square with concrete steps leading up to a small terrace and thence to the front door of the single storey building. We had arrived as the early tropical dusk was falling: a few Land Rovers were parked outside and their occupants were dismounting and making for the terrace. They were of various nationalities and were intent on some liquid to quench their thirst. They were the men and women of the many relief agencies that were busy in this impoverished country. They were polite to us but we were never able to get close to them. We got the impression that they looked upon themselves as the good guys with pure hearts, whereas we were trade, in it just for the money. The hotel was run by a Frenchman who appeared, at last, in the tiny lobby and showed us to our rooms. The two engineers, who were to stay here for six months, were given the first choice and picked the one with a shower and toilet, even though the shower was situated right over the toilet. Brian Jackson and I took the other room only to discover that it only had one bed, and that was a single. Brian is even bigger than me, vertically at least, and neither of us fancied sharing the narrow cot so we made a bit of a fuss. Eventually a camp bed was produced and placed at the foot of the bed. We tossed a coin and Brian lost. Exhibiting true leadership, I took the bed.

The manager showed us the public toilet across the narrow corridor and, by means of sign language, we were given strict instructions never to put toilet paper down the bowl, a tall basket was provided for that purpose. I could hardly believe my eyes, (or nose), and this remained the worst privation of my stay in that diarrhoea ridden country. Also, we were warned not to drink the tap water, and shown a filtering device that was definitely pre-war. We showered (in Jack and Tom's room) changed for dinner and went out onto the terrace to have a pre-prandial gin and tonic.

Our first shock was that there was no gin and tonic, beer was available tonight and, if the Dakota had managed to get back from Dakar, we might get red wine tomorrow. Guiné-Bissau had been presented with a bottling plant, of limited capacity, which produced, in rotation, beer, cola and an orange fizzy drink. All the drinks were in identical, unlabelled crown cap bottles of a dense green glass. As we spoke no Portuguese, and the barman spoke no English, drinking was something of a lottery. Knowledge of the plant's production schedule became useful. We settled for the rather thin beer and then walked round the square to investigate the attractions of the town. After one circuit, that took five minutes, we gained a small entourage of youths who followed us back and sat on the terrace wall and gazed at us, making comments on our appearances. We were the main attraction in Bissau.

Dinner was announced by dint of the other guests suddenly rising to their feet and charging the dining room. Dinner that night was a fair example of what we were to encounter for the rest of our stay. The first course was chicken soup we reckoned, after

The Douglas Dakota was a common sight throughout the continent of Africa during the 1970s. (MC)

a puzzled perusal of the fly blown menu. We were proved correct when a large, battered, metal tureen was placed on the table and Tom Cordener, who was a fussy eater, dipped an investigative ladle into the greyish contents. When he lifted it out there was a bony chicken leg balanced across it, feathers, claws and all. Tom refused to try it but the rest of us were not so fussy and helped ourselves. The main course was meat (that was as far as we got in our analysis), surrounded by unidentifiable vegetables. This too was tasteless and very tough. There was no dessert. From that point the evening went downhill.

The next day started early. Brian and I were woken by the sound of dustbins being overturned. I rose from my steaming bed (there was no air conditioning) and pushed open the shutters. There, in the street, were half a dozen enormous vultures examining the remains of last night's dinner. I closed the shutters hurriedly. We dressed and went out to sample breakfast. The coffee was not too bad and the tinned ham we found quite palatable, until we noticed that it had been cut into slices and laid out on the windowsill, where it attracted the attention of the local flies. Eventually, the airline bus arrived and we climbed aboard to begin our work. As we passed the President's palace, with its rows of red flags outside, I noticed that an ancient Peugeot taxicab sat on a small mound in the square. I had seen the same vehicle sitting on a similar mound outside the airport last evening. It took several days to find out that this car (the only taxi in town) had no starter motor and spent it's time running between the two mounds so that it's engine could be hill started when and if a fare appeared.

Our first task at the airport was to unload the aircraft. This took all day, due partly to the labour force observing union hours, however, the main hold up was that the only mechanical aid to our labour was a fork lift truck of doubtful vintage that had a decided list to port due to a flat tyre. No spare was available and no repair kit. We broke for lunch and retired thankfully to José's "office" at the back of the hangar. This small room had air conditioning, a great luxury, and became our retreat in times of stress. I cannot remember what we lunched on but we drank some of the Coca Cola that we had imported in the aircraft. It was contained in small screw topped bottles that, when empty, we cast into the waste bin with European carelessness. We later saw two cleaning ladies holding up some of the bottles and chattering excitedly. Apparently screw tops were unknown in Guiné-Bissau and the bottles became highly prized to hold cooking oil which was only sold in bulk (and after queuing for hours).

After lunch we resumed the unloading and eventually, when we were covered in grease and sweat, we reached the stage where only the spare Dart engine remained to be off loaded. We stood and regarded this monster with apprehension. I had witnessed it being loaded at Woodford by the use of half a dozen rollers cut from a length of steel scaffold tubing. I had told the foreman that I would appreciate it if they left the rollers aboard for use at our destination. He looked horrified.

"Not on your life, we need them here. Anyway, all you have to do is to get hold of some scaffolding when you get there and cut it up." Easily said in profligate Cheshire, but in tropical Guiné-Bissau anything resembling a length of scaffolding would long ago have been incorporated into the President's plumbing. We rooted around the aircraft and I found a tin of grease. We spread this liberally over the metal floor (and ourselves) and as many of us as could fit around it pushed and shoved the engine the length of the fuse-lage and up to the forward freight door, outside which waited the asthmatic fork lift truck. Despite my exhortations there it stuck. I looked out of the door and saw the reason, it was past four o-clock and the workforce was streaming across the tarmac on their way home. We decided to follow their example and, closing the door, we walked away from the aircraft towards José Pombo who had just landed in the only other serviceable aircraft in the country, a little Cessna 172. As he greeted us a messenger came panting up to him and handed him a slip of paper.

"It is from the President." José said with a broad grin. "There has been a bad accident up country and the President asks if we can fly to Quebo and bring back the casualties." There was, of course, no choice. The workers returned forthwith and with such strong motivation that the engine was almost lifted bodily off the aircraft. The engineers did a quick inspection, put in some fuel and the five of us, with José in the co-pilot's seat, set off for Quebo.

It was, by now, quite dark as we flew over the endless jungle with José navigating.

"What nav aids are there at Quebo?" I asked him.

"None" he said, grinning again.

"Oh," I said thoughtfully, "How will we know when we get there?"

"I will know it, I used to fly fighters from there before the liberation. It is by the river." José said, with more confidence than I felt. Later I asked,

"What lighting is there?" A sensible question as by now night had definitely closed in.

"Lighting? There is none. But do not worry, we painted the end of the runway white." José paused, "Of course, that was a long time ago."

Despite my doubts, José found the strip in the bend of the river, made visible by the moon reflecting on it. I flew over the dark clearing in the trees that José said was the air-field and, in our landing lights, I could just make out the white paint on the end of the runway. I lowered full flap, turned in over the tall trees and made a short landing on the very rough, crazed runway. I turned the aircraft round as tightly as I could because the runway was very narrow and the trees that I could see in our lights were extremely close. We taxied to the other end and turned again to face down the, by now, invisible runway. I shut down the port engine but kept the other one running, as I was not too confident of our battery capacity to do a restart. José got out of the aircraft and we waited.

After half an hour, during which time nobody had come near us, we saw lights appearing through the jungle. There were three Jeeps picking their way gingerly along the track. Each was loaded down with casualties on stretchers. Others limped behind the vehicles helped by soldiers and civilians. Apparently some big explosion had taken place several miles away and many had been hurt. We were to carry just those that need-ed urgent hospitalization. José came back aboard and sat beside me as the other three helped to settle the wounded in the seats or on their stretchers on the floor at the rear, for we had had no time to refit all the seats. Suddenly José jumped out of his seat and I saw him hurry back and pull injured people out of the seats and make them lie in the aisle. This seemed sensible, I thought, as they would be more comfortable lying down and I told him so when he got back into his seat and put his headset on.

"No," he replied, "They were bleeding on our new seats."

After much gesticulation I got the surrounding spectators away from the port engine and started it. I switched on the landing lights but they only served to make the gloom ahead even darker, illuminating only a mere 100 yards ahead of us. I applied full power against the brakes, released them and, as the speed passed 70 knots, pulled back and climbed as steeply as I could, not being able to see how much clearance, if any, I had from the trees ahead. We climbed up to 2,000 feet, breathed sighs of relief and set course for home. I asked José how long it would have taken to get the casualties to hospital by road if no aircraft had been available. I felt very humble when he said that there was no road and that they would have taken a week to get to Bissau by river, by which time they would almost certainly have been dead. We returned to the Grand Hotel feeling much better that night.

Over the next few days, I carried out the training of the other two pilots, José Castro, the other captain and Campos, a young first officer. The training went without major drama except for one night when the first officer was flying the aircraft on his first night flight

"They were bleeding on our new seats." The interior of a HS.748, depicting one of many seating layouts.

in the aircraft. I was in the right hand seat. All went well for the first hour or so until, during one circuit, as we were on the downwind leg, I looked up from reading out the checklist to find that the stars had disappeared. However, I could dimly make out in the moonlight the jungle tree canopy where the stars should have been. We were nearly upside down. Without the usual courtesy of "I have control." I grabbed the wheel and turned the aircraft back to upright. The First Officer's English vocabulary was improved that night.

We became thoroughly disenchanted with the Grand Hotel and asked if we could move to another hotel a little way out of town. This we did, but found that it was no better, just different. At least we now had rooms to ourselves. The hotel had been part of the

Portugese Air Force camp and the rooms were in huts a little way from the main building, which had been the Officer's Mess. These rooms once had air conditioning but now only had the hole above the door where it had once been. This hole now allowed in the particularly nasty mosquitoes. One evening, we sat on the terrace overlooking the huts and saw a bus pull up, from which descended a most elegantly dressed party of men and women. The barman told us that it was a fraternal visit from the Italian Communist Party. The party were shown to their huts and we waited, guessing what would happen now. We were right. Suddenly all the doors opened and out came the excitable Italians, all gesticulating and complaining bitterly to the management. Apparently, the reality of Marxist Leninism did not accord with Italian chic.

Guiné Bissau had been supplied with a few Mig 17 aircraft that lived at the far end of the airfield. I never saw them fly and thought them to be moribund. One evening, after the usual barely eatable dinner, I found a group of Germans sitting in the twilight outside my hut. There were two men and two women and I introduced myself and brought out a chair to sit with them. The two ladies spoke no English and the younger of the two men had very little. However, the older man, whom I judged to be in his sixties, spoke it fluently. It

The Mig 17 equipped several African Air Forces, however with limited spares and poor maintenance many shared a fate similar to Guiné Bissau's. (via OFP)

turned out that he was a pilot and had flown for the Luftwaffe during the war. I suggested that we might all like a drink. The ladies and the younger man declined but my fellow pilot readily accepted. I went into my room and brought out a bottle of Glenfiddich that I had bought in Lisbon. Under it's influence, the German pilot became firstly mellow and then started to talk caustically about communism in general and East Germany in particular. "Run by a bunch of stupid bastards", I remember being one of his phrases. The younger man began to shout in German and my companion shouted back, although his words were somewhat slurred. It now occurred to me that these were East Germans, not West as I had assumed. It seemed like a diplomatic time to say goodnight, anyway the bottle was now empty. I stood up and picked up the empty bottle and the cardboard tube it had come in. The two ladies now spoke to me for the first time and, by dint of gestures made it plain that they would like to keep the bottle and tube as souvenirs. I thought that this spoke volumes about the East German economy. I went to bed and never saw the party again. Perhaps their minder had shipped them back to the fatherland.

At some point in the middle of this period, my two engineers started to get a bit restless and Tom, in particular, was showing withdrawal symptoms for well-done steak and crème caramel, his invariable diet. We decided that we needed a couple of days of R and R in some luxurious watering hole. José Castro was by now up to strength so he acted as co-pilot to José Pombo and they carried out the first revenue earning flight to Dakar, in Senegal. A mere hour's journey. We four went along as passengers and booked into the Senegal Village Hotel for the weekend. It was unbelievably luxurious compared with the Grand; real showers, air conditioning and flush toilets. That, added to a topless beach and excellent restaurants nearby, made it a relative paradise. Tom Cordener indulged his Ulster taste for plain food to the maximum. One night he asked for a well done steak, but it came with red showing in the middle. He sent it back. When it returned it was just a little pink in the middle. After another two attempts to satisfy him the Chef suddenly burst through the kitchen doors and, to the clientele in general, announced in broken English, "I cook it no more!" and flounced back through the swing doors. When we got to the sweet Tom fancied a crème caramel with a vanilla ice cream. I studied the menu, (as the only one with any pretensions to speaking French) and, whilst crème caramel was easily recognized, vanilla ice cream was missing. There was something called an Eskimaux and we agreed that this would do. The waiter, with a flourish, placed in front of Tom a crème caramel with an iced lolly stuck upright in it. My reputation as a linguist never recovered.

At long last the training was complete. All that was left was for me to ride as shot gun on a freight run to Las-Palmas in the Canary islands with José Castro and our inverted First Officer flying the aircraft. Our load was to be 10,000 lbs of frozen fish, the first production of a new freezing and processing plant presented by the Russians. Mrs. Castro was to accompany us and Jack Howard was to be the engineer. We were due to leave at ten in the morning but by two o-clock nothing had happened. We were just about to give up when a large truck arrived with much ceremony, backed up to the aircraft and it's load was transferred. 10,000 lbs of frozen fish does not take up much room and the aircraft looked quite empty. We set off with me sitting on the jump seat and very soon the aircraft began to feel pleasantly cool. We were only dressed in lightweight shirts and slacks and, living in the tropics as we were, we had no heavy clothes with us; just a change of shirt or dress, in Mrs. Castro's case. As we reached cruising height I indicated to Campos that he should increase the cabin heating a touch. He showed me that he had already done so, up to maximum. The temperature continued to fall so I leant across him and pulled the choke lever to cut in the extra heat normally only used in the Arctic. It made little difference. By the time we landed at Nouhadibouh to refuel we were blue with cold. When we finally arrived in Las Palmas we resembled Tom Cordener's Eskimaux. A good night's sleep in a decent hotel, however, brightened up our spirits and, whilst Mrs. Castro went Christmas shopping, the rest of us went to the airport to file our flight plan and to supervise the loading of the 10,000 lbs of freight that José Pombo had arranged to be delivered to us.

We were sitting in the cockpit chatting when the freight arrived. At first we were merely pleased that it had arrived on time but gradually we began to have misgivings. More and more baggage trucks rolled up until a long queue of them waited alongside. It looked far too much to be contained in our little 748. José Pombo had negotiated the freight by weight and we were now the proud possessors of 10,000 lbs of blankets, towels, bandages and many other lightweight but bulky goods. The loaders did their best but they were unable to cram it all in. After over an hour of pushing and prodding they still had three whole truckloads left. The entire fuselage was full, apart from the cockpit, where we three pilots sat, and the very back of the cabin where Jack and Mrs. Castro sat squashed into the only two seats on board. The two ends of the aircraft were totally isolated apart from the intercom. However, the two in the rear did have one distinct advantage; they had the toilet back there. José paid off everyone who held out a hand from an enormous mill wheel of notes of various currencies. Nevertheless, as we started to move a fuel tanker was driven close under our nose and we came up all standing; we had not paid the loaders.

Eventually we got away and it was much warmer this time. In fact, the cooling system could not cope with the extra insulation and for this return trip we sweltered. At some point between Nouhadibouh and Bissau I realized that I had to go to the toilet. I held on as long as I could but nature was not to be denied and I had to find a way to get to the other end of the aircraft. I examined the load that blocked my way, and found that the port side of it was fairly loosely packed. So, lying on my side, I swam my way through a mass of soft, cuddly materials until I finally burst through into Jack and Mrs. Castro's cocoon. There was no Mrs. Castro! Had we left her behind? No, even worse, she was in the loo!

All the way back to Bissau I was nervously checking the time. I was booked onto the weekly Caledonian Airways flight, due to leave at four o-clock, to return to England home and beauty. I made it by the skin of my teeth. José Pombo and the rest of the airline staff were there to see me off, and my luggage was swiftly transferred from 748 to 707. I said goodbye with many regrets. I had made good friends in that impoverished country. They had so little to give but they were such nice people. I climbed aboard the 707 as the last passenger (again), and turned at the top of the steps to wave. I looked out at the jungle pressing in on the airport, the sun-baked hangars and the one and only taxi descending from it's mound and chugging up the Swedish road. I turned and smiled at the be-tartanned air hostess.

"A large gin and tonic please."

I got back to Manchester on the 22nd of December, in time for Christmas after all. As I waited to get off the plane the air hostess said brightly,

"Please mind the ice on the steps." I was home.

Overleaf: HS.748 G-BFVR of Linhas Aéreas da Guiné Bissau airlines with the author and José Pombo at the controls in December 1978. This particular aircraft was subsequently re-registered as J5-GAT. (Harry Holmes)

LINHAS AÉREAS DA

BISSAU
G-BFVR

Chapter Three

So You Want To Be A Salesman

On joining British Aerospace I found that the essential difference between being a test pilot in the services and being one for a commercial company is that in the latter case it is necessary to sell your product. If you wish to be paid you must earn for the company at least your own salary each year. I quickly learned that everyone is a salesman; the shop floor worker is often the most influential salesman of all when visitors are being shown round. Similarly, the test pilot, when demonstrating the product, can have an enormous influence on the sale. The best professional salesmen recognize this and use the test pilot accordingly. My introduction to the art of emulating the swan (all smooth on the surface and paddling like hell underneath), was in 1978. It was under the supervision of a test pilot who had been with the company for a long time, Harry Fisher, or Big H, as he is known, on account of his height and his voice.

Harry and I were briefed by Charles that a new airline was opening up in Andorra. It was to be based at an airfield called Seo de Urgel. The airfield was not yet finished but our sales team assured us that the strip available was 1500 yards long and had a good gravel surface; quite adequate for our purposes. One small twist was that, although the airline would be registered in Andorra (it's first ever airline), the country was so tiny that the airfield had had to be built just over the border in Spain. I read up all I could about the small state and found that it had been semi-independent since 1278 and came under the joint suzerainty of the President of France and the Bishop of Urgel. (During the demonstration we met the Bishop but the President of France pleaded a prior engagement). Apart from the fact that it was very mountainous and about the size of Macclesfield that was all I could find.

Present day view of Seo de Urgel which is now only used by light General Aviation. (David Roura)

Harry and I set off for Barcelona in G-BDVH, our 748 demonstrator, with Sue Tomes as our hostess, two engineers and a few salesmen on board. Ken Edgerton, the Chief Salesman, had gone on ahead and would be waiting for us in Barcelona, we hoped. We arrived in good order and, before leaving the airport, tried to prepare the aircraft for the next day's flying. This is when I learnt my first lesson about demonstration flying, stay flexible. Typically no one knew what was happening tomorrow. Ken Edgerton was in Andorra talking to the principals and would not be back until later in the day. Harry, although not surprised by the lack of information, was not forgiving. Several junior salesmen felt the rough edge of his tongue. We needed to know when we would be departing, how long we would be flying for (to take on sufficient fuel), and how many passengers we might be carrying. Nobody knew. We would have to try to do it all in a rush in the morning. With bad grace Harry arranged for a bus to take us all to the hotel and we left the airfield. Ken Edgerton did not appear until dinnertime. He held a briefing and at last things started to fall into place, helped by a superb bottle of Rioja bought for Harry and I by Ken. I remember his eyes watering when he saw the price.

The next day we hustled around and managed to get airborne by mid-morning. Our first problem was to find the airfield of Seo de Urgel. It was not easy. We had on board a representative of the putative airline and he taught me lesson number two; never listen to the local expert; he was more lost than we were. However, by some basic navigation we found a "White" mountain we had been told about and, by it, we saw a pimple of a hill with some quarrying going on on top of it. There were two cars there and, beside them, a small windsock. Unbelievably this was our airfield. The contractors were in the process of flattening the top of the hill and had half finished it, the southern half. At one end of the intended runway there remained a large lump of rock some 100 feet high, that protruded over the unfinished landing strip. We circled the airfield and talked about it. Harry reckoned that he could just

Another view of Seo de Urgel giving an idea of the kind of terrain surrounding the airfield. (Javier Ortega Figueiral)

about squeeze past the lump of rock in a slight curve to land into wind, which was a brisk westerly. He asked me to keep a sharp eye out on my side, the side with the rock on it, and give him a running commentary on how close we were. He came in on a curving approach, selected full flap and held the aircraft at threshold speed all the way in. I, meanwhile, had my face up against the right hand side screen saying inane things like "Looks good - OK my side - Should be clear." I had no time to think what would happen if I said, "Whoops, back a bit". Anyway we missed the rock and Harry set the aircraft down on the gravel surface and braked to a halt. The view ahead was not reassuring; where the strip ended it fell away over a cliff-like slope. However, we had made it and we were to make it several times again that day as we carried the airline representatives around the area, showing them how comfortable the 748 was and how it would be ideal for their purposes.

At the end of a long, sticky day Harry and I were sitting in the front two passenger seats, sipping a large gin and tonic each, before being driven to the local hotel where we were to stay overnight. The duty salesman had assured us that there were no more joy rides to be flown today. We had only drunk about a mouthful when the said salesman put his head through the front doorway and announced,

"Harry, sorry, but we've got another ten people out here with tickets. Can you do just one more trip?"

Harry's face spoke volumes. He looked at me.

"If we do it quick the gin shouldn't have an effect. Come on then."

We climbed back in our seats and did one more, very fast circuit and landing. Did the gin have any effect? - Nah!

As we drove to the hotel the duty salesman spoke to us very firmly. We were entertaining the prospective customers in a restaurant in Andorra that night. Our hotel was in Spain, just two miles from the border. It was vital that we took our passports with us. His talk bore fruit. Only one person forgot his passport, the salesman. He crossed the border in the boot of the hired car, there and back. The dinner was memorable for several things. The size of the joints of lamb on our plates was enormous. The four of us in the crew reckoned that we could have re-assembled the animal between us. We ate in front of a fearsome open fire that would have been welcome in winter but was unbearable in September! What really finished off the evening however, was when a Spanish gentleman sitting opposite Sue Tomes suddenly produced a hypodermic syringe and, with an apologetic smile, opened his shirt and plunged it into his belly, between the entree and the desert. Sue put down her spoon and ate no more.

The next morning, whilst the aircraft was being inspected by the customer's technical advisors, we, the aircrew, were given a guided tour of the parliament "Building". It was, in fact, a farmhouse and our guide, whom we took to be a caretaker, turned out to be the Prime Minister, part time. I still have the little hexagonal pot given to each of us that commemorates Andorra's 700 years of autonomy. It stands on the kitchen dresser and holds the household keys.

That afternoon we took the entire Andorrean parliament for a sightseeing flight; all of them, on a 48 seater aircraft! The aircraft could not have accommodated even just the British Cabinet. We flew around for half an hour or so, showing the MPs their small but delightful country; I, doing my best to give a running commentary. We then returned to the airstrip where, unknown to us, the freaky mountain wind had changed completely round and was now a brisk tail wind. Harry did his usual immaculate short landing and, just as I was relaxing, he exclaimed, "We're not stopping!" I did not ask him what he meant; I merely stared ahead to where someone had left a large bulldozer in the middle of the strip (We found out later that the driver had gone home and taken the key with him.)

Seo de Urgel terminal building and tower, sadly never used in any capacity. (Javier Ortega Figueiral)

As the earthmover grew ever larger in the windscreen the Members of Parliament began to applaud. Harry did manage to bring the aircraft to a halt, avoiding the bulldozer and just short of going over the edge of the cliff. Our extra ground speed due to the tail wind and the loose gravel surface, had combined to produce the alarming effect. Whilst I was very relieved that we had stopped I could not help laughing at the surrealism of the thought of an entire Parliament applauding it's own demise as it plunged over a cliff.

So ended my first demonstration tour. We never did sell any aircraft to Andorra but I learnt some valuable lessons. I treasure one gem of a comment from a salesman. I was sitting beside the hotel swimming pool with the same young salesman whom, the night before, had forgotten his passport. He turned to me and said very seriously,

"You know Robby, I don't think that I am cut out to be a salesman. I don't drink much and I sunburn very easily."

Although many of my sales tours took place in civilised places, an aircraft such as the 748 that sells on its versatility and ruggedness has to be demonstrated more often than not in the more primitive parts of the world. This meant that I often found myself in freezing snow, tropical rain or scorching desert. In 1980, I was flying our 748 2B demonstrator, G-BGJV, in Sweden and, on returning, had to continue straight on to the Oman, staging through Nice, Athens, Larnaca and Dubai, arriving in the capital, Seeb, two days later. We spent the next four days flying in and out of desert oil strips trying to sell the aircraft to Royal Dutch Shell to replace the Fokker F27s of Gulf Air. JV was quite a new aircraft then and it was impressive for grimy oil workers, who had spent a month in the desert, to be welcomed aboard an air-conditioned airliner with taped music playing and to be offered iced drinks by an attractive red headed Hostess, Sue Tomes. Normally women were not allowed at the oil strips and I had to negotiate special dispensation for Sue. The authorities made her an honorary man. I think they envisaged trouble from the sexed starved oilies, but Sue had no trouble. Alan Thompson, our young engineer, however, was pinched and propositioned several times. The Arab gentlemen concerned were discouraged in forthright Lancastrian terms.

Overleaf: HS.748 Series 2B demonstrator G-BGJV. The livery on this aircraft was very eye-catching, the upper forward fuselage was in red and the rear fuselage and tail was blue, complementing the British Aerospace logo. (Harry Holmes)

BRITISH
AEROSPACE
74
G-BGJV

Demonstrations usually took the form of working the customer's routes as efficiently as possible and giving flying displays when asked. It was hot sweaty work in the cockpit and Dick Muir, the co-pilot, and I drank many cans of coke as the day wore on. At Mamul, a sand strip well to the south of Seeb, I gave one such display, enjoying the freedom of an arena with no obstructions or other aircraft to avoid. I gave the audience a full ten minutes of short take offs and landings and steep wingovers into fast fly-pasts, and taxied in to the usual applause (Probably in relief at not having been on board). By now, I was bursting to visit the toilet but there is one inviolable rule in demonstrating, staff do not use the aircraft loo. It smells towards the end of a long day. So, as I came down the aircraft steps, I looked around for a likely spot but, as far as the eye could see, there was absolutely no cover except, perhaps, in the far distance where I could just make out a very small hut.

"Aha" I thought, "Even if it's not a loo I can hide behind it." So I set off across the burning sands in my natty airline Captain's uniform and gold braided cap. The hut was further off than I thought and, by the time I reached it, I could scarcely contain myself. As I fumbled to ready myself my eyes fell upon a small, neat notice on the side of the hut. It said in Arabic and English, "This is a Mosque. Do not urinate here." Collapse of stout party. I cast modesty to the winds and solved my problem in the open but well away from the mini-mosque. When I arrived back at the aircraft I could tell that, despite all our hard work, we had lost the sale. The Managing Director of Royal Dutch Shell,who had climbed aboard to see the facilities, had leant on the baggage poles, the paint on which had softened in the 120 degrees heat. His very well cut safari suit had great black streaks down it's back. None of us told him but I am sure that, when he got home, his wife dared him to buy such a messy aircraft. He bought Dutch F27s.

The Fokker F-27 Friendship was the HS.748s main competition in the short medium-range commercial transport market. (via OFP).

In September 1980, we set off on a mammoth sales tour of the USA to try to break into that difficult market. We left Woodford on the 29th, although we had planned to leave on the 12th. On that day I had arrived at the airfield all packed and ready to go. As I drove past the aircraft parked on the pan I could see that all was not well. Albert James, our engineer, and Tom Saunders, the senior salesman, came across to me. Tom was a shattered man.

"I don't believe it. I do not believe it!" he said, smacking his brow.

"Let's have a drink."

"Tom," I said, "It's eight o'clock in the morning."

He led me round to the other side of the aircraft and, with a shaking finger, pointed at the starboard wing. It was blown up like a balloon. Piece by piece I got the story. Something (subsequently found to be a rivet mandrill), had blocked the vent valve in the fuel tank in that wing. When the hangar staff had pressure refuelled the aircraft the wing had just inflated like a tyre, splitting the skin away from the ribs.

It took two weeks to repair, working day and night, and the sales staff also worked overtime sending a flurry of telexes to delay their carefully crafted schedule. Nevertheless, we made it, and late on the 29th we set off across the Atlantic the pretty way, via Reykjavik in Iceland, Sonderstrom in Greenland and Sept Isles in Canada.

Winter was already signalling it's arrival when we reached Reykjavik and we hurried across the light dusting of snow that covered the grey volcanic soil between the aircraft and the Loftleider Hotel. I took a much-needed shower and went down to meet the others in the bar. It was closed! I stamped back to the reception desk and demanded to know why. The tall, cool blonde behind the counter smiled mechanically at me "It is Thursday", she said, "No liquor in Iceland on Thursdays." I retired hurt.

The next morning, Dick Muir, who was my co-pilot yet again, Tony Wilson, the young salesman, and I had a good sustaining breakfast. We strolled across the, by now, hard frozen pan to where Albert James and Tom Cordener should have been refuelling the aircraft, having borrowed my fuel payment carnets the night before. There was no sign of them. I climbed into the aircraft and there found Tom crouched in a seat in the freezing cabin looking very ill. He had been up all night with chest pains and gave every appearance of having had a heart attack. I overrode his protests and wasted no time in calling for an ambulance to take him to hospital. I asked Tony Wilson to stay behind with Tom to look after any problems and telexed Woodford to let them know. The rest of us pressed on.

The next stop, Sonderstrom was, as usual, icy and I called for the de-icing truck to spray the aircraft. We filled the fuel tanks to the brim with the very expensive fuel and I went in to the small operations department to pay. The bill was for many hundreds of dollars and I reached into my pocket for my carnets. They were not there. I knew immediately where they were; in Tom Cordener's jacket pocket, hanging behind some hospital door in Iceland. I tentatively offered my personal American Express credit card. "That will do nicely." said yet another tall, cool Scandinavian blonde. I had to repeat this at every stop until we reached Washington where I could pick up some more carnets. I telephoned my wife and told her not to faint when she got the account and not to pay it.

Some days later, a letter arrived from AMEX inviting me to apply for a gold card. They thought that they had ensnared a really big spender.

The US tour was a success in every way except that of actually selling any aircraft. We visited dozens of big and little operators at airports with romantic sounding names. There was Poughkeepsie, Paduca, Ozark Lake, Raleigh and others with not such romantic names, Lynchburg and Carbondale for instance. The owners of the airlines were a tough breed. They were all pilots of some sort or other and had borrowed heavily to take advantage of the recent deregulation that had opened up the business. At Carbondale one such hard-bitten gent greeted us and took us downtown to a local hostelry where he poured whiskey and beer down our unresisting throats. Just as we were about to make our excuses and to go to bed to prepare for the morrow, he looked at his watch, stood up and said,

"Okay fellahs, it's midnight. The night shift will be in now so let's show them the aircraft." We smiled thinly and climbed back into the bus to go down to the airport. The night shift was indeed waiting for us so we pushed the aircraft up to the open hangar doors to give the engineers some light to open up the cowlings and inspect the goods. I spent the next two hours showing people around our shiny new aircraft and then we pushed her back onto the pan and refuelled her for the next morning.

"See you at eight." Said our host.

At Lynchburg, we visited an airline that had already bought the 748, so our visit was a relaxed occasion. We had come to let the airline show their new aircraft to their potential customers ahead of delivery. Also, we were going to entertain them as a thank you. I was prepared to enjoy myself and was pleased when the airline's boss said that they had organised the party to be held in the upstairs restaurant of the small airport terminal. The aircraft was to be parked on the pan just below the balcony. It sounded like a fun night. However, he went on to say, that he had told the guests that they could fly in the aircraft during the party. So Dick and I spent the night carrying ever more merry passengers around the local area. We, of course, remained totally alcohol free and got less and less amused as drunks pushed through onto the flight deck in a burst of noise and a waft of booze to make funny pilot jokes and to offer us glasses of various liquors. Never mind, after the last flight Sue Tomes presented me with a pint pewter mug filled with champagne cocktail. I am looking at that mug now on my shelf and the taste comes back to me.

We visited Lynchburg several times over that next few years until, unfortunately, the airline collapsed, as did many of the hopeful companies that had expanded under deregulation. They were under capitalised with no guaranteed routes. Most of our visits were uneventful, however, one visit there produced a small drama that made the local paper. As usual our salesman had arranged for me to give a flying display at the small municipal airport. I contacted the airport manager, a rotund ebullient character who always wore a ten-gallon hat. His name was Colonel Jesse Moorehouse and he assured me that he would close the airport for ten minutes whilst I whirled around. About three minutes into my show, as I pulled up into a wing over, I looked over my shoulder to get my bearings and there, where I would have been in ten seconds, was a small twin-engined aircraft flying over the field. I modified my routine to allow the other aircraft to land and, after we got down, I metaphorically gripped the egregious Colonel by the lapels and asked him what gave.

"Well hell!" he said, "That was Senator Bird. I couldn't stop him from arriving, could I?"

Apparently, Senator Bird was a very important gentleman whose demise was preferable to his wrath. I met him later that day at a lavish reception and he took it all in good part. Somewhere I still have a copy of the next morning's local paper. Under a photograph of the good Colonel was a headline saying:

"I told him no acrobatics!" says Colonel Jesse'

If you had asked Tricia, my wife, her favourite place on earth she would unhesitatingly have said Santa Barbara, California. She and I flew out there by Laker Airlines where I was to test fly the first 748 completed by Tracer inc. who had won the contract to fit out all 748s for sale in the USA. Tricia, together with Betty, the wife of John Lewis my co-pilot, and Joan, the wife of Mike Turner, the engineer, spent a glorious week in the Santa Barbara Inn whilst their husbands slogged away in the midday sun.

After completing the production flight test schedule on the aircraft, I was to renew John's Certificate of Test for the 748. I asked for the water methanol to be topped up. This is a mixture of methanol and de-mineralised water, carried in two small tanks in the wing roots. It is injected into the engines to boost the power for take off in hot conditions. It would be needed on this test when I would cut one of the engines on John as the aircraft reached take off speed. We set off along the runway at full "wet" power and I took good care that my hand did not stray to the high-pressure cock to give away which engine I was going to fail. In fact, I only made up my mind when we had started to roll. At V1, I grasped the starboard HP cock and pulled it back to feather. That engine duly stopped and John coped beautifully, putting on full opposite rudder and holding the aircraft at the correct speeds as we climbed slowly away. We continued the check ride, restarting the engine and carrying out a single engined overshoot, this time with the port engine failed but with the starboard at "dry" power. John passed the test and we landed and parked at the hangar. A mechanic came out to the aircraft carrying a large plastic barrel marked "Water methanol" and, as we passed by, he unscrewed the cap of the starboard water meths tank. Immediately both of us reeled back as an acrid rubbery smell hit us. We went round and checked the other tank. This time we smelt just the normal water meths smell. I ordered that the liquid in the tank and in the barrel be analysed. Later that day I was told that it was a butyl compound, used as a rubber solvent. If that had reached the engine it would undoubtedly have exploded, leaving us with no engines at all if I had chosen to cut the other engine on take off, or if, on the overshoot, I had not chosen to do it "dry". In flying you need a bit of luck now and again. Meanwhile, the wives were lounging in the swimming pool. We nearly spoilt their entire week.

One further memory of the USA. We were doing our duty in Houston, flying parties of very influential potential customers around and, after landing, I went down the back to thank the passengers for coming and to help hand out the give-aways that we had with us. I presented to a blue rinsed matron a key ring with a Rolls Royce logo on its tag.

"There you are madam," I said, with an ingratiating smile, "It looks good to leave around with your Ford Pinto keys on."

She gave me a frosty glare and moved on. Her obviously long-suffering husband took the ring from me.

"My wife drives a Rolls Royce." He said, with a sad smile. I saw it later, parked next to *his* Rolls. I was out of my league.

Over the years I have spent a lot of time in South America, in particular in Columbia. My first time was on a solo liaison visit to SATENA. This was a government run airline operating out of Bogotá that had been flying 748s for a number of years. The airline was manned by Air Force personnel and was headed by a full Colonel, Col Diaz. Our local agent, Ernesto, drove me out to the airline offices in his ancient Volkswagen, christened 'Hitler's revenge', and on the way he told me that one of the airline's 748s had crashed the week before. This was news to me as I had been travelling round the USA for some days, out of contact with Woodford. Consequently, I was ushered into Colonel Diaz's presence with some misgivings. After the usual pleasantries I was given a cup of the delicious coffee ever present in Columbia and the Colonel fixed me with glassy stare.

"So, Captain, you have heard of the crash of one of my aircraft last week?" I nodded guardedly.

"We do not know the cause." He went on, "It crashed into some hills to the north of Bogotá."

We discussed the circumstances of the crash, such as the time of day, the weather etc, until I eventually asked the big question.

"Were there any survivors?'

"No" was the reply, "But of course only one man died."

I toyed with the idea of asking if the rest of the victims were women and, if so, did this not reflect badly upon Colombian chivalry, but he went on to explain.

"This mechanic stole the aircraft and we think that he was showing off to his mother who lives in the flats near the crash. And, Captain, I would like to know how British Aerospace is going to help?" He eyed me closely and waited for me to reply to this seemingly answer-less question.

"Well," I said slowly, "I could teach your mechanics to fly."

He began to smile, then roared with laughter and slapped me on the back. The ice was broken.

My times in Columbia took me to a variety of strange places whose names keep coming back to me as I hear of the drug problems in that country. In particular Medellin, a beautiful city high up in a bowl of wooded mountains. Operating from there in the frequently foggy conditions was always difficult even in the 748, let alone in the Boeing 707s that were so popular there. It never surprises me to hear of crashes at that airport. As you spiral out of there to gain height to climb over the mountains it is quite usual to see trucks out-climbing you on the steep mountain roads that lie a mile or so off your wing tip. On various visits to the city I was always a little nervous that we might be demonstrating to drug barons who saw the 748 as an ideal smuggling tool. One Medellin airline official, when flying with me over the scrub and desert in the north of the country, said that they called this Indian country. I asked him why that was.

"Look down there," he said, "Cherokees, Apaches, Senecas..." I looked down to where he was pointing and saw the wrecks of those types of aircraft and more. Smuggler's aircraft that had crashed when overloaded with drugs. I could also see very long strips of cleared land and asked what those were. He told me that they were airstrips hastily cleared for the drug runners to operate from at night. Aircraft as big as 707s had taken off from these, ditching off the USA coast, the drugs being recovered by divers. The pilots were apparently very well paid; one flight and you could retire. "There's not enough money in the world to tempt me." I thought, and I still feel that way.

Now that I lead a more prosaic life my thoughts often turn to the more exotic parts of the world that I have flown in. I have no regrets and I have no wish to return to most of them. However, there is one spot I would go back to tomorrow; a place that I fell in love with, both with its scenery and its people; that jewel in the Indian Ocean, Madagascar.

HS.748s at Woodford awaiting delivery to Bogotá in Columbia for the military operated airline SATENA. (Harry Holmes).

Chapter Four

Madagascar- How it should be

In 1979 I carried out my first sales tour as Captain in charge. It was particularly memorable, not only because it went so well, but also because it was in Madagascar, that big, beautiful island in the Indian Ocean, populated by pleasant civilised people. The sales team was particularly well chosen and the tour took place at a time when the newly elected British government was trying to repair the diplomatic damage done by it's predecessor when it withdrew our ambassador in the name of economy. The auguries were good and we felt that if we lost this one we would not be lightly forgiven. Already in Madagascar was John Schofield, my favourite salesman, my co-pilot was to be Kevin Moorehouse and our engineers were to be Race Pilbrow and my old friend from Guiné-Bissau, Tom Cordener. The senior salesman was to be Tom Saunders, who had been one of my Instructors at Cranwell, and he was to be accompanied by Duncan Fraser, BAe's representative in Africa. Others were involved but my memory grows dim. It was one of those teams that comes together as if by design and immediately becomes a close-knit unit.

We all met some weeks before the tour and were briefed on the personalities we would meet and the envisaged operations. In particular we were told about the types of airfields into which we would have to operate. This caused us some thought, as the majority were extremely short rough fields, varying from soft grassy coastal strips to high altitude rocky pastures. One, Diego Suarez, even had a railway right across the strip. I asked for a train timetable. Hard information was difficult to come by and our calculations, as to the fuel and passenger loads we could carry, had to be based on very gross estimates. I had been introduced to the Madagascar purchasing team some weeks before when they visited Woodford. I was pleased to see that I would be demonstrating to a member of that team that I had taken an immediate liking to, Colonel Raymond Rakatonirina. He was the President's' aviation adviser and, as I later found, a pilot of great ability. (To everyone from the President to the aircraft cleaners he was Colonel Raymond, a very pleasant convention in Madagascar where names are so long that everyone uses first or nicknames). All in all we felt well prepared and motivated.

The first phase of our adventure was not reassuring. Our own demonstrator aircraft was not available and it had been arranged that we would borrow one that had been in service with Williamson's Diamonds in Tanzania. Willie Diamonds had assured us that it was in good order and, according to servicing and modification documents held at Woodford, it was. However, the reality was somewhat different. Kevin and I and the two engineers flew out to Dar-es-Salaam, courtesy of British Airways, on the 27th of May and expected to fly 5H-WDL to Madagascar on the 29th. The passenger flight out was uneventful and, as we flew close to Mount Kilimanjaro, it served to remind me that I was back in the 'Dark Continent' with all it's glories and frustrations. After arrival in Dar and after the endless business of waiting for our luggage in the steamy, fly blown terminal, I walked round the courtyard outside, where all the airline offices were, until I came to the Willie Diamonds office. It was closed. I walked back to the terminal and we argued our way on to the pan hoping to at least see our hired aircraft. We were told that it was away up country at Madui, the airstrip at the Willie Diamond's mine. (I made a mental note to check it's tyres tomorrow for diamonds).

We could do nothing else but retire to our hotel where we knew the company's Chief Pilot and his wife lived. We hired two taxis and set off for the Bahari Beach Hotel. On the way I saw that Tanzania, whilst not in a great state of repair, was infinitely better off than Guiné-Bissau. It was growing dark and it had been raining. The damp, wood smoke laden air of Africa was very evident as we drove along the main road to the coast. We passed lush trees and bushes and a lot of lying water. Cooking fires could be seen outside huts on the side of the road. At last we came to the gates of the hotel compound. Driving past a lake outside the fence we could hear a loud chorus of mating bullfrogs that boded ill for our sleep. The gates were swung open by armed guards. (Tanzania suffered from a spate of attacks on hotels by marauding armed gangs and secure compounds surrounded all the best hotels). The Bahari Beach was a comfortable billet, (I say "was" because it burnt down after we left). It was right on the beach and you could hear the constant pounding of the surf on the shingle. At least the noise of the sea masked the sound of the copulating frogs. We showered and changed and met in the bar, which overlooked the tropical sea. I sipped a local beer and felt that life could be worse. I was right. It got worse quite quickly.

The Scottish Chief Pilot and his beautiful Greek wife arrived as we were sitting down to dinner and over a very welcome meal we discussed the lease of the aircraft. Thinking to flatter I mentioned that Willie Diamonds' aircraft had been chosen as it was in such excellent condition. I should have been warned by the Chief Pilot's slightly evasive manner that all was not as it should be. He told us that it was due a Certificate of Airworthiness flight test in the morning but that it would be available to us after that. I organised my forces. We would all go to the airfield first thing, meet the local engineers and inspect the aircraft. Tom and Kevin would then stay with the aircraft, to do what might be necessary, whilst Race went to customs to check through the spares that should have arrived on the same aircraft that we had flown out on. Meanwhile, I would go to the Civil Aviation Authority offices in the city to negotiate the validation of our licenses and the extension of the aircraft's C of A to cover our intended demonstration program. Quite straightforward, we should be in good shape to depart the day after tomorrow.

We arrived at the airfield early the next morning and the day started on a low note and went downhill from there. Willie Diamonds was not happy with the terms of the lease and my first port of call had to be to their head office in town to smooth that over. We ran the local engineer to earth in his "office" in the Presidential Flight's hangar where the President's and several Airforce 748s lay in various states of disrepair. The engineer, Mr Singh (a turbanned Sikh whom our engineers immediately christened Jam Butty), gave us a tale of woe about his lack of spares as we sat sipping his excellent tea, and waited for 5H-WDL to return from it's C of A flight. It was being flown by an Airforce pilot, Major Wilfred M' Wutafunga, (who was given a nickname I will not repeat). Eventually we were told that it was on finals to land and we went outside to greet it.

Overleaf: HS.748 5H-WDL as operated by Williamson Diamonds Ltd. (Harry Holmes)

5H-WDL

It looked quite nice externally, glinting in the morning sun with the Willie Diamonds logo on the tail. However, the effect was spoiled by the fire extinguisher foam covering the wheels and by the fire engine following close behind. It turned out that the brake pads had been so worn that when Wilfred had braked hard on landing they had worn completely away and the metal-to-metal contact that resulted had produced a minor fire. We obviously needed new brakes, but luckily some were included in our spares. So we had no problem there, did we? Wilfred came to a halt and invited us aboard. He was a well-educated, urbane officer who straight away established that he would be coming to Madagascar with us. This was news to me and I politely said so. I wanted no interference with the demonstration and I suspected that he merely wanted to go to Madagascar on a jolly. I tucked this problem to the back of my mind for the present. We looked around the interior; it was all very tatty. The aircraft showed every day of it's ten years in service. Mechanically, it was all right but it was in no condition to be shown as an example of British Aerospace's products. My first action was to telex John Schofield in Madagascar telling him of the situation and suggesting that we delay the demonstration until our own aircraft was available, a matter of two weeks or so. He replied that he could not delay it that long but would delay it by two days. I had to accept this and we set out to try and make the aircraft presentable. We began by begging, borrowing and stealing from the Airforce who were absolutely charming and readily lent us, at no charge, all we needed; all, that is, except new brake units. As a thank you, I promised to persuade BAe to give them a windscreen for the President's aircraft, which had come off worse in a bird strike.

Whilst all this was going on, I presented myself at the offices of the Department of Civil Aviation and began my wait. To this day I cannot see a SANYO advertisement without being transported back to that depressing corridor. I spent all that afternoon and most of the next day staring out of the window at a giant neon sign of the SANYO trademark. However, it was all worthwhile, for I was eventually ushered into the presence of a senior civil servant who could not have been more helpful. I was, after all, asking for a lot. I was proposing that I take a Tanzanian registered aircraft to a foreign country, toss out paratroops and fly Farnborough type displays when requested. Furthermore, I was asking that Kevin and I and the two engineers be issued with permission to exercise the rights of our British licenses in that foreign country. Proposed amendments to the Flight Manual had been produced by Bob Dixon-Stubbs, our Flight Operations Manager, and I handed these over. The large, urbane gentleman shook my hand, offered me tea and sat patiently whilst I talked at length. He studied the amendments and then, with a gentle smile, said:

"You are a test pilot?"

"Yes I am."

"Well, I am sure that I can, in that case, rely on you completely. I will have the necessary letters of permission ready by the end of the day. However, I am afraid that Major M' Wutafunga and Mr Singh will have to accompany you."

I accepted with good grace. I had been given more than I expected and I recognised that Wilfred had outmanoeuvred me.

I took a taxi back to the airport in high spirits only to find gloom and despondency in the team. They had been told that our spares had not been on our flight, nor on any flight since. I set off for the customs office taking with me Race Pilbrow, who had local knowledge, having served here some years before. The scene that greeted us looked like a tropical version of the Retreat from Moscow. All was chaos. Packages and crates lay all around and, among them, sat disillusioned applicants. Behind a rickety counter stood a brooding official, shaking his head at the besieging hundreds around him, all waving forms in his face. Race beckoned me to follow him and led me through a side door into the bonded warehouse where a mountain of packages reared up against the far wall. We picked our way towards it, past crates containing long lost imports and started to search through the mound. Soon, with a cry of triumph, Race found a package addressed to us and then we found another and another, until we had all the items on our list. With a little bribery, Race managed to get an official to come and inspect our pile. He shrugged and stamped our papers. We had our spares, including the biggest prize of all, four new brake units, without which we could go nowhere. Two more days work and we were ready to go.

We coasted out on a southeasterly heading, climbing to our cruise altitude. As this was the first time that we had flown the aircraft, I gently weaved it around to feel it out whilst Kevin checked all the radios and other equipment. I noticed that the fuel low temperature warning light was standing proud. I leant forward and screwed it in. It came on! Surely the fuel could not be too cold so soon after take off? I unscrewed the amber light out again and it stayed that way for the rest of the tour. The aircraft flew well. It was a good example of the 748 whose best characteristics are ruggedness and good handling qualities. Wilfred and Mr Singh were asleep down the back whilst Tom and Race tidied up the aircraft around them. We settled down and cruised out over the Indian Ocean, past the lush jungle on the coast and white sands shading into ever deepening blue sea. Eventually we could see the Comores and flew past looking down on the hilly little islands to our left. On the main island I could see a very good-looking airfield on the southern shore. Later on, BAe was to visit there and try to sell the 748 to the local entrepreneur.

Madagascar appeared on the nose. A very large piece of land, bigger than the UK. We could see the hot, tropical coastal strip that gave way to steep foothills leading to a central plateau rising to over 7,000 feet. We crossed the coast at Majunga, the airfield from where the RAF had operated to patrol the Beira Straits during the Rhodesian UDI confrontation. Towns were few and far between but we could make out rice paddies and the pastures where the Zebu cattle grazed. It looked a pleasant land; there were even vineyards in the fertile valleys. The Capital, Tannanarive, came into view with it's international airport. We took particular interest in this airport as we would be based here and would have to fly several displays over it. It looked good. The only possible problem was a rocky ridge to the south, close to the runway and parallel to it. It only rose to some 300 feet higher than the airport and, in normal operations, would be no problem, in display flying, however, it would be a hazard that I would have to be aware of and, if possible, use to my advantage. The field was surrounded by rice paddies and several small lakes. We flew past once and then landed and taxied into the terminal and up to the Air Madagascar hangar. It was obvious that this was no primitive African airline. This was a sophisticated operation. Outside the large, well maintained hangar stood a variety of aircraft with the airline's logo on their tails. There was a Boeing 747, two 737s, several Twin Otters and numerous smaller aircraft. These gentlemen would take us to the cleaners if we tried to pull the wool over their eyes.

Air Madagascar operated a single Boeing 747-200 for many years. This aircraft is presently in storage.

As we stopped the engines, the greeting party advanced towards us. In the lead were Tom Saunders, John Schofield and Duncan Fraser, all looking much relieved. Behind them was a party of airline officials, whom I had not yet met, and the patrician figure of Colonel Raymond. We climbed out of the aircraft and were introduced to the members of the party, one of whom was the British Chargé D'affaire, André Marcellin, a tall Mauritian with shiny black skin, an impeccable Oxford accent and Saville Row suitings. He was to become our friend and saviour on several occasions, one of which arose immediately. It was found that Mr Singh was travelling on an Indian passport, with no visa. André had solved the problem by the end of the day, but it cost us some of our reputation for efficiency.

After clearing customs, I was taken to the airline offices where I found a large meeting waiting for me. I was immediately put in the hot seat. Their Operations Director set out the program for the demonstration and passed me a list of airfields that we would use. Each airfield had printed alongside it the length and nature of the runway. He fixed me with a serious stare and asked me if I would be prepared to operate into the airstrip called Besalampy. As I looked at the airfield data, which gave the length as 1,000 metres and the surface as grass, he went on to say that the Dutch pilot of the Fokker F27, who had demonstrated to them last month, had refused to land there. It was news to me that Fokkers had preceded us but I recognised that I could lose the battle here and now with the wrong answer, I glanced at the faces of our salesmen and could see the strain behind the smiles. Why had the Dutchman refused I wondered? I put on a brave face.

"Of course I will" I said, "I see no problem. The 748 is built for strips like that."
Relief all round; general talk broke out and, in a spirit of camaraderie, we repaired to the Hilton Hotel.

On the way into town, a journey of some fifteen miles, I was fascinated to compare this country with the rest of Africa. It became immediately obvious that it was not part of

Africa. Some of the people looked like those of Mozambique or Tanzania but the majority looked more like the inhabitants of Colombia or Ecuador. I later found that these were the two distinctive races in the Island. The former were from the tropical strip on the west coast and the latter inhabited the high plateau. Even the traditional dress and music of these people were very similar to those of the South American tribes. The road wound around pastures and paddy fields and through village markets that came right up to the edge of the road and where our bus had to thread it's way through a busy animated throng around the stalls. The houses were a mixture of small French style bungalows and a few, very old, high eaved, thatched buildings with wooden walls; looking like pre-revolution French cottages. As we came into the city we could see evidence of a sophisticated society; suburban housing, parks and several small guesthouses. The Hilton Hotel did not look out of place as it rose above the surrounding buildings to some twelve storeys.

I booked into my room on the tenth floor and looked out of the window across the city. Opposite was a large ornamental lake in a public park, above which rose a steep cliff. On top of that could be seen the palace of Queen Ranavalona who, in the nineteenth century, executed thousands of her subjects each day by having them walk the plank out over the cliff to be dashed on the rocks below. Apparently, her official birthday used to be celebrated by a special effort when the executioners raised their annual productivity rate. I hoped that this quaint old custom no longer applied. I showered and dressed and went to the lift to descend to the bar and a much longed for gin and tonic. I waited and waited. Eventually I gave up and walked down the stairs, all ten flights of them. I later found that the lifts failed to work several times a day and, when they did work, were full of small North Koreans and their minders. In the bar the rest of the party mingled with khaki clad, tough looking, freedom fighters from Rhodesia/Zimbabwe on rest and recuperation. In this mixed company we raised our glasses to success and looked forward to a couple of weeks that promised to be at least interesting.

The next day, the first of June, started bright and early with a demonstration flight to Colonel Raymond and several airline representatives. It took the usual form; half an hour of smooth, quiet flight followed by half an hour where I let the local pilots do their worst. Colonel Raymond quietly insisted on occupying the right hand seat right from the start. Kevin therefore had to sit on the jump seat between us and carry out his checks as best he could. I tactfully explained to the Colonel that I would do all the flying for the first half of the flight and that I would be employing a few non-standard procedures so as to give our passengers as smooth a flight as possible. He grinned and readily agreed. He realized that one has to present ones product to it's best advantage, without actually cheating of course! Passengers do not like noisy aeroplanes but it is the change of engine note that alarms them so I always made as few changes as possible. We lined up on the long runway and I let the aircraft trundle forward as I eased the throttles forward until we had 14,200 RPM instead of the usual 15,000 that the Dart uses for take off. I let the aircraft raise itself from the runway, cleaned up and very gradually turned on to our desired heading, keeping the power constant. We levelled off at 12,000 feet (6,000 feet above the ground) and I put in the autopilot, gradually reducing power until we were oozing along nice and quietly, much below our usual cruising speed. As I did this a small young man called Desireé leant over Kevin's shoulder and remarked that the take off run had been longer than forecast and that the cruise speed was some twenty knots below the brochure figure. Hoist by my own petard! I had come across my first example of Madagascaran realism. Their philosophy was "To hell with noise and comfort - how many passengers can we carry and how fast can we go?" I gave up, selected full cruise power and promised Desireé that I would give him a full performance demonstration when we got home.

The second half of the flight went well, as it always did. The 748 is a superb pilots aircraft, it handles beautifully and is vice free. Raymond was surprised that I sat back with my arms folded and let him do the take offs, landings and full stalls without ever touching the controls. Apparently, the Fokker pilot never allowed this. He threw the aircraft around in steep turns and I encouraged him to stall it with one engine feathered. He thoroughly enjoyed himself and I felt that if he had been the only man to make the decision we would have already won. We made the final landing and the sales team ushered the passengers off.

I was now due to give a display and, for this, I insisted that Kevin be given back his seat. However, Colonel Raymond stayed on the jump seat; a brave man. We made a very short take off and I turned steeply to keep the aircraft low so as to disappear behind the rocky ridge I had noted to the south. I reappeared round the corner to roar over the spectators at 50 feet and to pull up into a steep climbing turn. This sort of thing went on for another five minutes before I ended by making an ultra short landing, selecting high drag on the propellers just above the ground and braking heavily. Thank God for those new brakes! We taxied in to a round of applause and to pick up members of the press who were to write up the visit. We flew the reporters and cameramen around for twenty minutes. This time I let Colonel Raymond do all the flying, from the left hand seat, which made for some fine photographs of him at the controls and was good for a few column inches in the next day's papers. The day ended with a meeting with Desireé and his colleagues on the matter of performance and, as it was time for tea, we returned to the Hilton to prepare for the next day's VIP flights.

The VIP flights consisted of a nice simple program; flying to Tamatave, the island's second city, on the east coast, flying another display there and bringing our passengers home. These flights went without a hitch, unlike another VIP flight some months later. Among the party on that flight was the Minister of Transport, a fat, jolly little man of shiny black aspect. We had taken the high ranking group to an up country town where they had wined and dined with an intensity that I had come to accept as the norm in Madagascar. The other pilot on this outing was Andriam, the airline's Chief Pilot. He and I, as usual, had to sit and sip fruit juice whilst those around us emptied many bottles of the excellent local wine and several of Scotch, to which they were addicted. On the return flight they were still in high spirits and kept themselves topped up. As we approached Tannanarive at dusk and entered a zone of fearsome thunderstorms, one of the Minister's entourage appeared on the flight deck and announced in sepulchral tones:

"Excuse me Captain, the Minister has just died."

I have previously explained the meaning of the phrase "making like a swan"; this announcement really tested my savoir-faire. My feathers were definitely ruffled. I unstrapped and went back down the cabin to where a small knot of, by now, very subdued men and women were bent over the figure of a very dark blue Minister, lying prostrate in the aisle. The Hostess had found and administered the therapeutic oxygen but the Minister remained blue and unbreathing. I said a few well-meaning words and returned to the flight deck where I called ATC for a priority landing and for an ambulance to meet us. Andriam raised his eyebrows at me and we threaded our way through the thunderstorms and landed. We taxied in, neither of us speaking, and quickly parked and cut the engines. We sat in silence for a few seconds waiting for the man-made storm to break around our ears. Suddenly the door flew open and the "dead" Minister appeared, grinning hugely.

"Sorry to upset you Captain. Thank you for an excellent flight"

He and his party disappeared into the terminal and we never did find out what really happened. However, this delight awaited me in the future. The present flights, as I said, went without a hitch.

The next day, June the third, was another day of VIP flights, this time to Nosy Bé, a delightful tropical island off the north coast, famous for it's Lemur colony. We lunched at the Holiday Inn and swam in the beautiful blue waters off the perfect, white, deserted beaches. Lunch was served on long trestle tables under the palm trees and consisted of fish baked for hours in a pit in the sand and many varieties of local vegetables and fruit. The principal guests were the British Consul (a German businessman called Herr Plusmacher) and his tall, stately wife. André Marcellin and Herr Plusmacher did not see eye to eye, he described him as suffering from proctalgia, but their state of armed neutrality did not spoil this delightful occasion. One day I hope to go back to Nosy Bé. It is the perfect holiday spot. We flew back to the Capital in high spirits. Tomorrow the real work would begin.

This was the real crunch day. Today we were to put the 748 into some very short, nasty strips; varying from soft, sea level meadows to steep, high altitude, rock strewn fields. The names of the airfields were musical: Majunga, Soalala, Besalampy, Tambohorano, Maintirano. They covered the northwestern part of the island and we were to fly them in the order I have written and then to return in reverse order back to Tannanarive. At Majunga, our first stop, I was scheduled to carry out a display, so I was interested in the airfield layout so as to fix in my mind my turning points and, most importantly, the height of the surrounding terrain. I circled the airfield on arrival and quickly took in it's geography. It was a coastal field with a good tarmac runway of ample length but it was hemmed in on both sides by steeply sloping tropical jungle that came down close to the runway's edge. The pan, where the passengers were to stand to view the display after I had dropped them off, was at one end of the runway and built back into the trees; not an ideal layout to display the aircraft to it's advantage. However, I did my best and threw the aircraft around in even steeper turns than usual to keep it in the spectator's sight. The bravest men on the flight were the two engineers. The 748, when empty of passengers, needs some 500 pounds of ballast in the tail compartment to bring the centre of gravity within limits. We had not been able to carry any ballast with us on this trip as, on the short strips, we needed all our carrying capacity for our full load of passengers. The engineers volunteered to become human ballast and, throughout the display, crouched in the rear baggage hold, with no windows and with no means of me communicating with them. Really trusting I thought.

Typical Madagascan airstrip. Note the primitive but effective way of displaying the wind direction.

I picked up my passengers, amongst whom were the Governor of the Region and his retinue. They were to fly to the airfields in their area of responsibility and were to have a say in the final choice of aircraft. Colonel Raymond was still in the right hand seat and down the back was an Air Madagascar steward and stewardess who were to serve drinks and give the safety briefings. The stewardess was Colonel Raymond's daughter, and very pretty and efficient she was. Our next stop, Soalala, came into view and it looked quite good. It was right on the coast and even had a sealed runway, that was dirt sealed with bitumen or oil. It was very short and surrounded by trees but all in all it looked no problem. On one side of the field there appeared to be a gravel path, halfway along which was a small white chimney with a fire lit at its base. From the chimney issued white smoke, which blew diagonally across the runway. I remarked to Colonel Raymond that it looked as though a new Pope had been chosen. He told me that there was such a chimney at most of their fields. There was no radio or telephone so a man was employed to listen out for approaching aircraft. When he heard one he lit the fire and threw on some green leaves to make smoke and thus to indicate the direction of the wind. A simple idea that worked well. I over-flew the field, turned onto a left base leg to keep the touch down point in view all the time and lowered the undercarriage and full flap. I held the speed at a few knots over the required threshold speed in a fairly steep descent, aiming at a point just inside the runway. As we crossed the threshold a couple of feet up I cut the power and pulled back sharply to cushion the touch down. I selected ground fine, the high drag propeller angle, and braked hard, Colonel Raymond holding the control column fully back as requested. We stopped well within the runway length and turned round to taxy back to the packed earth area beside the chimney that served as the parking pan. I spoke to the passengers on the PA, thanking them for travelling with BAe, and the stewards opened the doors and lowered the air stairs. Just like a real scheduled airliner. Our passengers alighted for a few minutes and then we were off again.

Besalampy was our next stop, the field that the Dutch captain had refused to land at. I looked down at it with some apprehension. I could see what he meant. It was rough. The runway, if you could call it that, was natural surfaced and muddy. Tall trees came to within 50 yards of the runway ends and sparse but high undergrowth came right to the edge of the extremely narrow strip. I could see that the main problems would be avoiding becoming bogged down and trying to turn round once we had stopped, the 748 is quite a big aircraft, having a wing span of 100 feet. Nothing ventured nothing lost, (except perhaps face, if we became immovable in a mud patch). I did the normal short landing and we stopped well before the end. I tucked as far over to the left of the strip as I dared, with the propeller on my side chopping at the tops of small bushes and saplings, then swung it round on full lock with the right hand brake full on and the left engine at high power. The aircraft slewed round and we were facing down the runway again. I would have to do this all over again at the other end, but before that we encountered the first large mud patch. With a sinking heart I felt the aircraft slowing down even though I was increasing the power. I pushed the throttles through to full wet power and the aircraft reluctantly struggled out of the mire. The passengers again alighted and stared around them laughing and pointing. We had obviously scored a point. The take off was quite normal, if sluggish, and we went on our way.

The rest of the day was relatively uneventful except at one high, short airfield where I had told the salesmen that we could only carry 36 passengers to achieve the necessary performance. In reality the aircraft could have carried a full load out of there and, using military criteria, would have done, but civil regulations restricted our take off weight. Many of our original passengers had left us here and as I waited for our new passengers to board I chatted to Colonel Raymond, who was clearly having a great time. Because of this I did not notice the scrum taking place in the cabin behind us. The door warning light went out and I started the engines. As I turned onto the rocky runway John Schofield fought his way forward and peered over Kevin's shoulder.

"How many passengers John?" I said.

He looked a bit worried. "Fifty two." He blurted out.

Kevin and I glanced at each other. We only had 48 seats in the cabin. "Think swan" I thought and opened the throttles. There was, of course, no problem about the take off but, down the back, Tom Saunders sat on the toilet and John Schofield and the two engineers walked about to conceal the fact that they had no seats.

Day five of the demonstration was to be a military day. The 748 is capable of dropping both stores and paratroops. We were to show off this capability by dropping 22 free fall parachutists. Jumping from the 748 has one particular hazard in that the tail plane is low set and quite close to the doorway. If you are foolish enough to jump out in the first place you need to adopt a fairly precise attitude to avoid bouncing off the tail plane. To instruct those about to commit this foolishness we normally employed the services of Bob Ackerman, a grizzled veteran of many hundreds of jumps. Unfortunately, Bob was busy but he had sent one of his associates, Graham Snooks, who was also very experienced but who looked fragile and young. As we readied the aircraft Graham stood on a flat bed truck and lectured to a group of the toughest, most hard-bitten paratroops you have ever seen. They thought it hilarious that they were being told how to jump out of an aeroplane by such a beardless youth, but they put up with it with good humour and went through the motions as instructed. One thing that they did admire was Graham's high tech parachute and jump suit; such luxury was completely unobtainable for them and they stood round stroking them and murmuring to each other.

We loaded up and took off, gradually climbing in a spiral to 12,000 feet. After depressurising the aircraft, I signalled for the engineers to open the freight door. I leant across to look down the fuselage to where Graham was marshalling the troops and gave him the thumbs up. Air Traffic cleared us in and, with flaps down and holding the aircraft level at 100 knots, I called for the red light to be put on to warn the jumpers that we were on our dropping run. As the chosen pasture disappeared under the nose I asked Colonel Raymond to put on the green light. The whole thing was over in thirty seconds and, after the last man (Graham Snooks) had gone, I winged over to spiral down round the fallers. You could see the small dots rushing earthwards until, one by one, the chutes opened; one, two, three...twenty-two khaki coloured canopies and then, finally, the brightly coloured square para-wing that denoted that Graham's had also opened safely. I breathed a sigh of relief and turned for home. A nice, easy day, and that night there was to be the inaugural meeting of the Anglo-Madagascan friendship society that was to take the form of a party and dance. Something to look forward to. I expected to see Graham Snooks back at the hotel but, on the way home, an army lorry full of our jumpers pulled out in front of our bus and there was his grinning face in the middle of them. All were in high spirits and Graham was now obviously very popular. In fact, his new friends entertained him rather well in the more disreputable parts of town and we did not see him for 24 hours. His parachute and jump suit never did reappear.

There remained three more days of demonstration; one of them consisting of carrying round a party of high ranking army officers intent on seeing if the aircraft could be used to supply their outposts in the mountain. We were to land at several strips but, in particular, at one grass field high up in the Massif du Tsaratanana, the mountains to the north of the country. The big problem was to find the field and, to this end, the top brass had appointed an Air Force Major to help us. Colonel Raymond had chosen to travel down the back with his colleagues on this occasion so Kevin was back in his own seat and the Major knelt between us. Although it was a nice sunny day in the mountains, there was a lot of turbulent cumulus cloud around the tops and the approach to our destination necessitated weaving in and out of the towering white masses, flying close to the green sugar loaf peaks. As we came round the shoulder of one of these peaks we hit, without warning, a wind shear that gave us the biggest jolt that I have ever experienced in an aircraft. It was so bad that the engineers down the back were convinced that we had hit a mountain and remained tightly curled up on the cabin floor where they had been flung. Even up the front I could hear the crash of breaking glass as the VIP's lost their drinks. I hastily throttled back and slowed down to reduce any further stress on the airframe and glanced at the Major. The sight that met my eyes reduced me to giggles; the Major was struggling up to his knees with a startled look on his face. His smart peaked cap had jammed itself over his eyes and had lost it's pristine white top so that the bamboo spikes that lay beneath stood up like a crown of thorns. Kevin began to giggle and the Major, after wrenching off his cap, saw the funny side of it and all three of us roared with nervous laughter. The engineers sheepishly climbed to their feet and cleared up the broken glass. I plotted another course to the strip and, after several fly-pasts to clear the Zebu cattle and to alert the small detachment there, we landed safely. Up until then only small, single engined aircraft had been able to land there so the Corporal in charge was extremely startled to find himself greeting the entire Army General Staff. I did not tell him how close he had been to instant promotion to General.

A fully trained crew pose in front of one of six HS.748s delivered to Air Madagascar.

Our final day of the visit was a return to flying the airline's routes, this time in the northeastern sector. One of the airfields on this route was on a beautiful island called St-Marie or Nosy Borah. This was a favourite holiday spot and the airport boasted a hard top runway and a small hut that served as the terminal. As with all but the four main airfields in the country, it had no radio and no telephone. It did, however, have the duty fire lighter and his chimney. On this occasion there was no mishap but the island sticks in my memory because of an event that took place some months later.

We had successfully sold six 748s to the airline and, whilst waiting for their delivery we were training their pilots and operating a schedule with our two demonstrator aircraft. On this particular day, I was training Marc Perrier, a French co-pilot, and Peter Henley was flying the line and had landed at St-Marie with a full load of 48 passengers. As I droned round the circuit at Tamatave, Air Traffic told me that Peter had called them on HF radio (a luxury not fitted in my aircraft) explaining that he had burst a tyre on landing and had no spare. We had a spare and a jack and an engineer, Joe O'Brien, so we set off to rescue him.

We landed on the small island strip to find that Peter had managed to taxy the aircraft off the runway to the small hut where the passengers waited in good humour. It was decided that the quickest course was for Peter to take our aircraft and continue on his way leaving Marc Perrier, Joe and myself to change the wheel on his aircraft and fly it back to base. The passengers and their luggage were transferred and Peter took off for Diago Suarez. I turned from waving him goodbye and saw Joe, helped by some local gents, starting to pump up the jack. As I watched, the jack broke through the thin tarmac crust and bent in half. Luckily, the aircraft, having two wheels on each leg, merely settled down onto it's one good starboard tyre, but we were now stranded; no jack, no telephone and no radio contact, as I found after calling plaintively on VHF and HF for several minutes. Joe and I looked at each other. It could have been worse.

The island was beautiful and the natives friendly. It was tempting to just stay there, however, duty called. I looked at the undercarriage with it's one flat tyre and it's one good one and had an idea. We cast around in the long grass near where some construction had been going on and found a concrete fence post. I was able to make the locals understand that I would appreciate some help to drag it to the aircraft. They talked about it amongst themselves for a while and appeared to be apprehensive. Eventually they started to poke about with sticks at the grass around my feet until, apparently satisfied, they ventured into the grass and lifted the post to the aircraft. When asked, they explained by signs that the grass where I had been standing was a favourite resting place for the very venomous local snakes! We pushed and shoved the post until it was lined up in front of the good tyre on the effected leg and made a ramp up to it with some of our gravel ballast. I climbed into the aircraft and started up. With the help of hand signals from Joe and Marc, I gunned the engines until I felt the wheel lurch up onto the post. Joe hastily signalled for me to stop and I braked heavily and cut the engines. The foot wide good tyre was now balanced on the six-inch wide post and the burst tyre was an inch clear of the ground. We were then able to change the wheel and beat a hasty retreat back home.

HS.748 of Air Madagascar. (Harry Holmes)

Our final day of the demonstration in Madagascar was the 6th of June. In the morning we flew yet another batch of VIPs around and made our farewells to all our friends who had come down to the airport to see us off. Colonel Raymond and other dignitaries shook our hands and gave us small presents. I presented Colonel Raymond with a bottle of Glenfiddich, his favourite tipple, and we climbed aboard. We climbed out again; two of our party were missing; Wilfred M' Wutafunga and Mr Singh. As we sat and waited our audience gradually drifted away, leaving only the crew to wait forlornly for an hour and a half, getting more and more irate. At last a small bus appeared and, in the middle of it's load of hi-fis, pottery and other goodies, we could see the beaming faces of Wilfred and Jam Butty. They had been shopping.

The McDonnell Douglas DC-10 prototype at the Paris Air Show in the early 1970s. The entire DC-10 fleet was grounded in 1979 after a series of fatal accidents. (via OFP)

Part of our anxiety at the delay had been that we were due to catch the British Airways DC-10 flight home that day. We need not have worried; the flight had been cancelled. All the world's DC-10s had been grounded after a series of crashes. (It was said that an Irish airline, not having any DC-10s, had grounded a DC-4 and two DC-3s). We were stranded and there were no hotel rooms available. A fitting end to what had been a most enjoyable sales tour. Our efforts were crowned some months later when it was announced that Air Madagascar had ordered six 748s and both Kevin and I returned to train the crews. Oh, and we did finally get home by dint of pleading, berating and bribing airline officials with BAe ties, pens and lighters.

Chapter Five

On Becoming Chief

I had been with the company for eighteen months when Charles Masefield, the Chief Test pilot, made me his deputy. He had been operating without a number two for all that time and it had been a strain for him coping with the overall company responsibilities of that post as well as the day to day running of the department. Charles also needed to play his part in the flying side of his job and to do that, he needed to shed many of the more immediate and minor tasks, such as running the flying programme. Apparently he had tried to appoint me six months previously but the board felt that they could not promote someone who had been with them for less than a year. However, this time they agreed and I was given the title of Deputy Chief Test Pilot and a company car!

After leaving the RAF, I had found myself in a very different world. I had exchanged one where I had been totally secure for one where I was no longer certain of the pecking order; an important fact for a serviceman. In the Air Force you can tell who is superior to whom by the stripes on their arms or the rings on their sleeves; a nice relaxed and simple way to order one's life. At Woodford, I quickly found that one had to walk round the back of a colleagues company car to see if his engine was bigger than yours, or if he had a Ghia to your GL. I soon became acclimatised to this but it complicated life somewhat. Now, being the proud possessor of a Granada 2.0L, I was on the ladder; only one rung up admittedly, but quite satisfied.

I had not been in the least dissatisfied with life in the RAF when Tony Blackman had head hunted me and I was reconciled to the fact that I was turning down the chance of promotion in exchange for the opportunity to go on test flying. I knew that I could never become Chief Test Pilot because Charles was ten years younger than me and was set to be CTP until well past my own retirement. Ambition had not died but had been modified. I settled down as Deputy and operated as such for the next year. It was therefore with utter surprise that I greeted Charles' announcement towards the end of 1980.

I was in the middle of training pilots for the German airline DLT, and also preparing for yet another sales tour in South America, when Charles called me into his office. He asked me to shut the door behind me, which was unusual in itself, and motioned me to sit.

"Robby," he said with a slight smile. "I'm to be made a Director. Norman Barber wants me on the board as soon as possible."

The German airline DLT bought six HS.748s, the first entered service in 1981. This is the demonstrator G-BGJV displaying the 'DLT' letters.

Norman Barber was, at that time, our Managing Director and was not a person to take no for an answer. In fact even a "maybe" would receive the reply "Pillock!" Charles really had no choice, even though he would initially suffer a drop in pay for the honour. (Time has proved Norman to be a good judge of character as Charles has gone on to be knighted as the Government's Director of Defence Sales and then to be a member of the Main Board of BAE Systems.) It did not immediately sink in that he was saying something of importance to me personally.

"So Robby" he went on, "Early next year you will become Chief Test Pilot." I had many mixed emotions. It was a big job that he was handing me. There were others in the department who would be hard hit by my appointment, for precedence showed that the deputy was not necessarily the heir to the Chief. I would have to become more closely involved with the plethora of problems facing a CTP, such as budgets, union negotiations and, above all, dealing with people's foibles and sensitivities. We talked at length about all these matters and many more. Eventually, after mutual congratulations, I left his office and went to continue showing Eckhart Geibelhausen and Harold Faecke how to fly the 748.

I could hardly wait to finish the day's flying and go home to tell Tricia the good news. I had to share it with someone even though Charles had made a point of saying that I should keep it to myself until it was formally announced. Tricia was delighted and said that it would be good to have me at home more often.

"Uh, yes" I said, "By the way darling, I have to go to South America next week."

The one person that I could talk to at work was Bob Dixon-Stubbs, our Operations Manager. He would be my right hand man in my future post and would suffer some of the inevitable backlash from the appointment. Meanwhile, he and I were to go to Washington and pick up G-BGJV (with which Peter Henley was finishing off the USA tour) and take it on to Ecuador. On the BA 747, as we flew to Dulles, we talked endlessly of the problems of running the department and of future changes. We were to continue this conversation in many hotel rooms over the next few weeks. Meanwhile, I was determined to enjoy what I thought to be my last sales tour and I intended to start my new job on a high note.

Bob and I entered the lobby of the Dulles Marriot Hotel where Peter and the rest of the party were celebrating their home going. Everyone was in high spirits except for Syd Blackshaw, the engineer, whom we found being helped down the stairs by Albert James. Poor old Syd (known as El-Syd since our Spanish exercise) looked awful. His face was swollen out of all recognition and he was on his way to hospital. "Here we go again", I thought. I seemed fated to lose engineers. They must have been getting short of them at home as even though Tom Cordener, who we had left in Iceland, had now recovered, he was still grounded. It turned out that Syd had a very bad case of infected gums so I had to send him home. It was all down to Albert again. We sat down with the departing team and began to swap gossip. They were full of their experiences and were avid for news from home. Peter Henley was particularly interested in departmental matters and it was very tempting to tell him my big news. However, I resisted and the next day the three of us waved Peter and the rest off and set off for Ecuador.

We customed out at Fort Lauderdale after spending the night there in the rusty roofed Holiday Inn yet again. The next day, the 30th of November, we coasted out over the Caribbean and flew south for five hours until we reached that jewel of Dutch possessions Curacao. Here, we refueled and left on our final leg to Quito. Our departure from Curacao had been delayed due to the lack of a fuel bowser and the usual airport niggles so we did not arrive at our destination until night was falling. The weather was less than the best. The airfield, which is at 15,000 feet altitude, had cloud cover over it at 500 feet above the ground and, as we approached, ATC announced that they were closing in five minutes time. As we flew down the ILS glide slope the Ground Proximity Warning System suddenly sounded. Just as we broke cloud it's dark brown, artificial voice called "Pull up! Pull up!". I had no choice. I had to overshoot. I glimpsed the runway lights so I stayed below cloud and turned sharp left to carry out a visual circuit. I turned left because, for one thing, it is natural for a pilot sitting on the left to do so, but mainly because I could see thousands of lights scattered over hills to our right whilst to the left there was nothing but blackness. As I turned I realised that the reason for the blackness was that there was a mountain there, very big and very close. I pulled very tight and opened the throttles to full power. Bob, doing his duty, said,

"Watch the TGTs." (Turbine Gas Temperatures), which had gone to the limit.

He received a very short reply, "F— the TGTs. Let's miss the F——g mountain!" Luckily we did and landed rather shakily. We saw the mountain the next morning and it looked very big and hard.

We stayed in Ecuador for a week of demonstrations and then flew on to Colombia to visit my old friend Colonel Diaz, the CO of SATENA. This was scheduled to be just a nice, relaxed one day visit to show the Colonel the 748 2B, in the hope that he would order this more powerful version of the aircraft to replace his aging 2As. Just two nights in Bogotá with no flying and then the long trudge home. Or so we thought!

The day of our arrival had been long. We had done two demonstration flights before we left Quito and we therefore arrived in Bogotá in the dark. As soon as we stopped the Colonel climbed aboard and greeted me like a long lost friend.

"Captain Robinson, welcome. I have made all the arrangements and tomorrow morning you will replace one of my aircraft on the routes. This you will do for three days."

I remonstrated but was left in no doubt that if I did not comply my clearance to leave Colombia would be mysteriously lost for several days. Bob and I were stymied, but we were faced with real problems. We had no Colombian licenses and the aircraft was on the British register. In the short time scale we had been given we could not take the necessary steps to make it legal.

We set off for our hotel in a very dark mood, which was not improved by the news that rooms that our local sales representative should have booked for us were not available. It was the last straw. I turned to the rep, who had accompanied us, and asked him where he was staying.

"I'm okay thanks." He said, "I have a room here. You might try the hotel down the road, they should have rooms."

"No," I said, "You try the hotel down the road. We will take your room." We mounted the stairs and entered the room. Whilst the rep packed his bags with bad grace I started to make the first of a long series of phone calls back to Charles Masefield in the UK to explain our position. Because of the time difference and the vagaries of the Colombian telephone system, it took most of the night to get the final answer from Charles, who had been working away at his end. The final verdict was that we had to go along with the Colonel and do as he wished. Bob and I went grumpily to bed where we got a whole three hours sleep before the bus called for us at 7.00am to go to the airport.

Bogotá airport is very prone to fog and as we got closer we accepted that we were going to be delayed on take off. The galling part was that we could have got another two hours much needed sleep instead of sitting in the cockpit waiting for our passengers. South American airlines pay only passing attention to performance requirements so we were expecting to be full even though we were replacing a 748 2A that should only have carried a reduced load of forty passengers. However, we were unprepared for the numbers of customers that wended their unsupervised way out to us across the tarmac as the fog cleared. I counted over a hundred souls and it suddenly came to me that we must have been replacing a SATENA DC-6, that could carry 100 passengers, and nobody had told the traffic office. I opened the cockpit door and was faced by a cabin where every seat was filled, the aisle was chock-a-block and more people were trying to squeeze past the hostess who was vainly trying to stem the flood at the doorway. Everybody was shouting and waving tickets in my face. I plunged in and, together with Bob, threw some 50 or 60 people off. We did nothing to enhance SATENA's reputation as Colombia's friendly airline in that half-hour but at least we managed to reduce the load to a mere 48 passengers, all with seats. Where their luggage ended up I never knew. We flew the three days for the Colonel and it was with some relief that we obtained our clearance to fly out of Colombia on our way home. Again we went the pretty way, via Panama City, Mexico, Florida, Washington, Canada and Iceland; from the equator to the Arctic Circle. At least this time I had my fuel carnets with me.

My promotion was announced just before the Christmas break, to take effect on the first of February 1981. Some feathers were ruffled, as I expected, but all in all it was well received and I spent my first day in charge with Maureen and Sue, our two secretaries, going over the files and trying to get into my head the mysteries of budgets and capital estimates. I also drove over to Chadderton for the first of my weekly visits to the Managing Director Norman Barber. The Chief Test Pilot worked directly for the MD in those days and therefore had to submit himself to these interrogations. Norman, a thickset, rugby playing extrovert, had a well-tried technique to reduce his subordinates to a co-operative jelly. He would sit in the darkest corner of his office and retire behind his heavy horn rimmed spectacles in total silence, until the interviewee could stand it no longer and would blurt out facts that he had had no intention of revealing. It was a very effective technique but I was an old hand at this having spent 28 years in the RAF being grilled by a variety of senior officers. I responded in kind and the two of us would face each other in impenetrable silence for minutes at a time. I think our relationship could be called an honourable draw. Never mind, I now had a Granada 2.8i GL!

Nimrod MR.2 XV260 on patrol over the North Sea.

In that first busy month my flying rate fell quite markedly. I only totalled eighteen hours in the air whereas in January it had been a respectable fifty-five. I note from my logbook that I flew G-11-15, a production 748 2B, on drooped ailerons and autopilot trials, a Nimrod Mk2, XV260, on production tests and the prototype Nimrod Mk3 AEW, XZ286, on handling tests. The latter aircraft gave me a nervous flight on February the 10th when Johnny Cruse and I lost two engines at high speed, but I run ahead of myself. My first problem as Chief was to appoint a deputy. I had no wish to run solo as Charles had done and I had some weeks before I made my mind up who it should be. I was a relative new boy in the industry and I needed an old hand beside me to cover the daily problems of running the flying programme. Johnny Cruse, I decided, was the right man. He had been at Filton carrying out the Concorde engine development programme, flying the Vulcan test bed with the Olympus engine underneath. He had joined Hawker Siddeleys at Woodford some years ago and was now the Nimrod AEW project pilot. A double load as project pilot and Deputy Chief Test Pilot might be unfair but I reckoned that he could handle it. He proved to be well up to the job and was invaluable as my deputy until his retirement in 1982, when Peter Henley took his place. I shall always be grateful for his support in those early days.

One of the things that I shall always treasure about my time at Woodford is my relationship with the occupants of the Flight Sheds. At BAe, at that time, the major aircraft components, such as the wings and fuselage sections, were made at Chadderton, assembled in Main Assembly on the north side of Woodford, and prepared for flight testing in the Flight Sheds on the south side of the airfield, alongside my department. I dealt with a series of inscrutable northern men in those sheds, who became quite scrutable with the passage of time. Men such as Jack Bolton, Albie Vernon, George Ward, Bernard Carroll, Billy Albinson, Billy McGeehan and many others. Jack I remember in particular because we would start the day with a slanging match about why the aircraft promised for today was not going to appear until Friday evening and end the day the best of friends.

All the pilots were very flattered to be invited to the Flight Sheds Christmas party at which the George Ward awards were presented to those who had dropped the biggest clangers over the last year. I sit here surrounded by those presented to me over the years, including a neat little ceramic owl mounted on a well-turned base. This was presented to me in recognition of my efforts to keep birds out of the hangars by putting large plastic models of owls in the rafters. The birds attacked them and built nests in the remains. The trophy is inscribed TWIT (TO WHO) AWARD". I got my own back by presenting

to Johnny Patchett, who looked after our ailing company Dove aircraft, the Noah's Ark Award, "For putting forth a Dove only once every forty days." The awards reflected the nature of our relationship, friendly insults covering great mutual respect. It has always been true that test crews rely completely on the integrity of the technicians who prepare the aircraft for flight and the technicians are very aware of this.

I not only had aircrew in my department but also Air Traffic Control, the Safety Equipment Section and the Crash and Rescue Section. The latter gave me more heartaches than most, not because of the people in it but because of the daily tight ropewalk of ordering and authorising overtime out of a limited budget to cover a very elastic flying programme. I tried

de Havilland Dove 8 G-ARHW in British Aerospace markings. The aircraft still survives, now operated by Pacelink Ltd at Fairoaks.

to pass this task off onto my deputy but it came winging back to me and it is one of those jobs that I do not miss. Another aspect I do not look back on with pleasure is my dealings with the Unions. Not that the officials were unpleasant, I got on well with them. The firemen's own representatives, of which there were several over the years, were always rather unwilling to serve and could never forget that they were, first and foremost, firemen. The biggest problem was that the men wanted to leave their present union that they thought of as being for ladies, and join the Firemen's Union. I, naively, thought that this was their right and nothing to do with me. However, I found myself the bad guy in an inter-union wrangle where the Bridlington Agreement on the non-poaching of members was shouted about. How I came to be representing the men I have no idea but it took up a lot of my time. I also upset the union by doing heinous things such as getting them pay rises and increasing the uniform allowance. I was encroaching on their territory. I was just doing what I had been taught in the RAF, looking after my people.

The crash crew had few opportunities to show their mettle, thank God. They conscientiously carried out their training every day and stood by for all the emergencies that are common in test flying. Mercifully, in my time, they were never called upon to deal with an aircraft crash but their keenness never flagged. This was partly due to the leadership of the Chief Fire Officer Alan Whittaker but mainly to the calibre of the men. Although they did not have to deal with any aircraft crashes they had to deal with many factory accidents. One particularly nasty incident occurred in 1987 when the roof of one of the hangars collapsed.

I was sitting in my office and felt a harsh tremor that I assumed was the hangar doors being shut with too much enthusiasm. Tony Hawkes, one of the test pilots, put his head round the door and said that the roof had caved in. I ran along the corridor and down the stairs into the hangar. The whole far end was open to the sky and a large pile of roof rafters and roofing sheets were heaped high and clouds of steam were spurting up through the rubble. A number of roofers had been working among the rafters renewing the insulation and these men had rode down on the falling timber. They were staggering around and stumbling out into the fresh air. The whole shambles was very precarious and a very dangerous place to be but the Crash Crew, who had already arrived, were digging frantically to rescue survivors. With no thought for their own safety, they dug and propped until they reached a man they could hear calling through the mess. Eventually, with great care, they extricated a man who had only joined us the previous week and who had been sitting eating his lunch at that end of the building. A ruptured high-pressure steam pipe had seriously scalded him and, as the firemen carried him into the ambulance, he asked us if he was going to make it. Of course we said that he would but sadly he died later that day. The hangar collapse also destroyed the Lancaster belonging to Charles Church the builder and aircraft enthusiast. You can imagine the litigation that followed. At least five parties sued each other and I do not think that the true cause was ever established; however, the bravery of the crash crew certainly was. When I retired I was very proud to receive from them a beautiful model of a fireman in full kit, a constant reminder of a rewarding relationship.

There is something in the northern man's psyche that hates throwing anything away and that loves to make do. Even the hangars at Woodford were bought secondhand by A.V. Roe himself in 1922. The Transport Manager, Jack Habberjam, was known as 'SecondHand Rose'. Our Air Traffic Control equipment was no exception and the SATCO, Eric Gladwin, was never slow to point this out to me. The height of our achievement in that direction was to get a new loo when Linda, our lady ATCO, joined us. Eric and I set to work to improve things and, over the years, managed to squeeze out of our masters new radar and radios and arrester gear to allow us to receive Buccaneers for refurbishment. The most difficult case to make, however, was for the replacement of the one and only ATC vehicle. We even managed to get a garage built to house it but the "yellow peril" hung on. It was a Mk 2 Cortina whose vintage was unknown as it had no number plates. Push starting was the norm and the daily runway inspections were hazardous, as, during the search for debris, it was likely to become a very large obstruction itself. It had wheels of different sizes and great ingenuity had been used to accommodate four hole wheels where five holes should be. It was suffering from terminal rust and finally Eric settled it all when, after it suffered a major structural collapse in the car park, he declared it unsafe to drive. We managed without one for a considerable time, using private cars for our daily needs but, after some cajoling Jack was forced to concede that we might have a case. We got a replacement in the form of an old Land Rover. It was a perfect replacement; reluctant to start, unreliable and it would not fit into the new garage.

Being close to Manchester Airport meant that our ATC had to liaise closely with the controllers there, and there was a constant battle of wits when we needed to carry out testing in the Woodford circuit. On the whole it worked well but it was a daily niggle, as was our relationship with our surrounding neighbours. Since it's opening in 1922, the airfield had constantly grown to accommodate ever-larger aircraft. In the forties it had acquired hard surfaced runways so that Woodford could deliver up to ten Lancasters a day to Bomber Command and, in the fifties, the main east-west runway had been lengthened to allow the Vulcan V bombers to be built there. This new extension crossed an ancient footpath and, British law being what it is, we could do nothing to close it, or even to just divert it round the end of the runway. It was a constant challenge to ramblers, especially at the time of the annual Woodford Airshow, when foolhardy citizens would encroach on the runway despite the efforts of the police. They resembled the sheep that also kept wandering onto the tempting acres of grass from our farmer neighbours to whom, I suppose, we seemed like upstarts who would eventually take the hint and leave.

Modern view of Woodford clearly showing the substantial factory complex on the north side of the airfield.

Considering the amount of noise generated by our activities, we received few complaints. However, we had our regulars. Not long after I took over as CTP I received a letter from a farmer who lived in the hills to the east of us, claiming that a Nimrod on such and such a day had been an annoyance over his farm. In fact he claimed that it had flown over "with all it's rockets firing". In the interests of good relations, and in a fit of new boy enthusiasm, I wrote back at length explaining the situation and that, in fact, I had been the pilot on that day and could assure him that we had been at a proper height over his property. I received further abusive letters from him over the next weeks, one stating that, "men like you should be shot!" Out of interest, I read back over the Noise File (a hefty document) and found quite a few letters signed by him, the earliest being dated 1956 when the then CTP, Jimmy Harrison, had started a round of correspondence similar to mine some 25 years later. The final letter on the subject at that time was from the farmer's son saying that "the Doctor says that dad is quite harmless" and promising to keep an eye on him. My last dealings with the gentleman were in 1982 when, at the height of our in-flight refuelling tests during the Falklands war, he appeared at three in the morning in his pyjamas at the main gates, where a startled guard refused him entry. I got a letter from him two days later saying that he had visited us to complain about the night flying, "Your man at the gate told me that you were refuelling in the air at night. I told him not to be so stupid as such things were not possible." I wish he had told me earlier and then we would not have done it.

An HS.748 of LIAT 'The Caribbean Airline' captured on a short island hopping flight. (Harry Holmes).

As CTP I spent most of my time firmly tied to Woodford. However, I still needed to get away from the admin now and again and what better than a trip to Antigua for a few days and a gentle flight home in a good old 748. Or so I thought! Al McDicken and I, together with Dave Atherton and Randy Sweeting the engineers, flew out by Eastern

Airlines on the second of January 1986 to pick up an aircraft that had spent many years flying for LIAT in the Caribbean. We intended to fly back to the UK via Bermuda and Iceland; about five days in all. Of course the aircraft was not ready. Never mind, we could have a couple of days lying in the sun on the glorious beaches by our hotel and sample the restaurants and bars in the evenings. This we did. Eventually of course V2-LIP was ready and we reluctantly prepared to leave. Snag one was that we found that the aircraft only had small fuel tanks, about two thirds normal capacity. We did not even know such 748s existed! This put a spanner in our works, as now we could not go the pretty route to Bermuda. We would have to crawl up the eastern seaboard of the USA and Canada and cross the Atlantic via Greenland and Iceland. This would take a week. I sent a flurry of telexes to Woodford but nobody seemed to have missed me. However, hidden in the replies was snag two. The aircraft was to be sold to a Philippines airline and part of the contract was that the LIAT logo had to be obliterated before leaving Canada. We put this problem to the back burner and plotted our route.

Our first landfall in the USA would be Fort Lauderdale, an airfield we knew well. However, we needed a staging post before that to refill our reduced tankage. We scoured the charts and chose North Caicos as our halfway-point. Snag three, there was no jet fuel on North Caicos, in fact there was a general shortage throughout the Caribbean. South Caicos, a tiny island ten miles to the south of the main island, however, claimed to have some left. On the 5th of January, we left Antigua and flew up the island chain in beautiful weather. The sea shaded from blue to green where the coral reefs stood out in the clear, shallow water. Several crashed aircraft also stood out, stranded on the reefs. We were, after all, close to the Bermuda triangle. South Caicos had no navigation beacon on it and as we let down the visibility became quite poor. We homed to the beacon on North Caicos and set off on the correct course hoping to see the small island. I should mention that the aircraft had no Distance Measuring Equipment (DME), so we had to time our approach, (this was to be a problem throughout our passage home). If we missed, and had to land at North Caicos, we would be stranded because of it's lack of jet fuel. Of course, as an anti-climax, we found the island with it's sandy airstrip and, after clearing the wild horses, we landed and refuelled. That was our major drama over, we thought.

When we reached Fort Lauderdale, Florida, we taxied into the space in front of the Customs post and shut down. No problem! A leisurely shower, maybe a swim, a meal and bed. Al and I entered the small building and stood before the counter. After a few minutes a tall, blond haired customs officer appeared and grunted at us. I smiled and explained that we were staging through the USA on the way to the UK. He was not friendly.

"You are importing an aircraft to the United States of America. Fill this form in and I require you to post as security one million dollars." One million dollars! My credit card would not cover that. I tried to convince him that I had staged through the USA many times before and had never had to do this. He was adamant. My only recourse was to contact a Notary Public and get him or her to post the required sum. It would cost BAe dearly but I was in a fix.

"May I use your phone please?" I asked,

"No, there's a public call phone outside."

"Can you change ten dollars into dimes then please?"

"No".

Al and I sifted through our pockets and found a few coins and I went out to the call box and began phoning. It was a public holiday. Every number in the book answered electronically, "I'm sorry but nobody is in the office today. Please try tomorrow. Have a nice day". After half an hour of this I returned to the customs post to throw myself on our hero's mercy. Al was standing right up to the counter with look of a Scotsman who is prepared to reopen the battle of Bannockburn. Opposite him was the, by now, yellow eyed customs officer who was equally pugnacious and was fumbling at his holster, luckily empty. I attempted to mediate without success but another customs man came out from the back office with a sheaf of forms.

"It's OK Hank. I've found a form called Permission to Proceed. I think that covers it". Our hero retreated muttering about "Goddamn Limeys".

As we proceeded up the East Coast, the temperature fell with the increase in latitude. When we landed at Norfolk, Virginia it was quite parky and our old aeroplane started to show it's age. The poor old girl had spent twenty years in the heat of the Caribbean and the fuel system seals now showed their disapproval of being rudely thrust into the cold of a North American winter. They shrank and fuel began to leak from every joint. The authorities at Norfolk Airport were very unhappy at our spreading jet fuel over their nice new tarmac and melting the tar. We incurred a fine and were told to leave as soon as possible. Our next port of call was Halifax, Nova Scotia and we knew that there was an airline there, Canadian Pacific, that flew 748s and would therefore hold fuel system spares. It took three hours to reach Halifax and no fuel gauges have ever been so carefully watched. When we landed on the snow- bound airfield we were leaking like a sieve. The temperature was twenty below zero so the first priority was to get the aircraft into a heated hangar and Canadian Pacific readily provided this, at commercial rates of course. The next priority was a stiff drink and bed. The local hotel provided these.

Work began in earnest the next morning. Whilst Dave and Randy began to dismantle the fuel system, Al and I started negotiations with the airline for the necessary spares. They gave us every help; albeit with a bit of horse trading to get some priority for the delivery of spares that they were waiting for from British Aerospace. The aircraft, of course, had to be de-fuelled as a first step. You cannot just suck out the fuel and put it into the normal underground tanks. It has to be treated as contaminated. Equally, local environmental laws prevent one from just discarding it. The only solution was to hire a fuel tanker, suck the fuel into that and hold it there until it could be put back into the aircraft again. This was expensive, but had to be done. Also it took much searching before we found a fuel company willing to do it. Eventually all was ready and Dave put us to work. We pilots were the donkeys, fetching and carrying for the engineers, including their laundry. They did allow us to do burner wipes; wire brushing the fuel spray nozzles, and putting them back into the flame cans. This entailed wire locking, an esoteric art that we got quite good at, but I well remember the anxiety of having our efforts inspected by Dave who often sniffed and said tersely, "It's anti-locked." Which meant that we had failed to put the wire in correctly and would have to do it all again. Our fingertips were shredded. The other task allocated to us pilots was the painting out of the LIAT logo, the task we had put off in the warmth of Antigua.

We drove our hire car through the deepish snow to the local town and marched into a paint shop. It was just a domestic paint shop, like FADS or Home Style, and the girl behind the counter was bored.

"What sort of paint?" she said, looking around at the full shelves.

"Um, well I suppose white gloss."

"How much?"

"That's difficult."

"Well, what are you going to paint?"

"An aircraft."

This got her attention. "An aircraft? Jim come out here."
The manager and several other assistants came out from the back of the shop and goggled at these crazy Brits. We eventually left carrying what turned out to be far too much paint, together with sundry brushes, rollers and a lot of white spirit. We knew what messy painters we were. We had to paint much of the top of the fuselage and, if one is painting it, the 748 is a big aircraft. It was hard work and took several days. Even then the letters 'LIAT The Caribbean Airline' showed dimly through. Good enough for government work though.

Exactly one week after arriving we were able to continue our Odyssey. Goose Bay, Labrador was our first stop. The winds on this leg were very strong, that we had known from the forecast, but in those northern latitudes one is never sure how strong it is in reality. Nevertheless, two and a half hours later "The Goose" appeared on the nose and we landed and refueled as quickly as possible before sampling the delights of the Labrador Inn, a hostelry of dubious quality that we had stayed at many times before. It provided, however, a welcome spot of heat in the surrounding snow. The lady behind the reception desk was her usual welcoming self.

"Have you booked?"

"I rang from the airport."

"Got no record of that."

"But I did. I asked for four rooms with bath."

"Sorry, I got no record."
I visualized a night in the snow. This was the only hotel in town.

"Well have you any rooms available?"

"Oh yeah" she said with a smirk," I got plenty of rooms."
Sadism was obviously her way of relieving the endless night in those high latitudes.

The next day began very early. It was due to be a long day as we had no wish to overnight anywhere in Greenland; just to refuel there and press on to Iceland. We planned to fuel stop at Gothaab, the capital town. In common with all the settlements in Greenland, it was at the head of a long fjord and its airport was built at water level on the side of a small harbour, with granite walls rising several thousand feet on either side. Our possible diversion airfields were Sondrestrom or Narssarssuaq, both some 200 miles away. We knew that we would have to make up our minds to divert before we descended to Gothaab so as to leave ourselves a safe fuel reserve margin to either. Never mind, the weather forecast was fine and the forecast winds not too bad even though they were on the nose. As we flew north, we tried to calculate the actual winds but radio aids on the route were few and far between and it was not until we saw the coastline on our radar that we could check our true position. Of course, sod's law held good. Not only was the head wind much stronger than forecast but also the weather at Gothaab was much worse than we had been led to expect. There was an ILS but it had no glide slope transmitter. The cloud base was just on limits but only with a working DME. As I said before we had no DME in the ancient aircraft. There was an NDB/ADF radio beacon at Gothaab but it was out in the fjord some way from the airfield and anyway the cloud was lower than the limits for an ADF approach. Al and I debated. The possibility of reaching either of our diversions was, to say the least, doubtful with our depleted fuel and the weather at both was marginal. Our only real choice was to land at Gothaab. We timed ourselves from overhead the NDB beacon and began our descent on the ILS from where we hoped the correct descent profile began.

The wind above the granite cliffs was a howling sixty knots but below the cliffs it was about twenty and from the opposite direction. The wind shear created some nasty turbulence that was to continue throughout the approach. As we sank into the clouds I girded my loins and concentrated hard on following the wavering ILS needle and holding the imaginary glide slope that I had estimated would bring us to the airfield, if we had started our descent at the right place. Al sat beside me saying nothing, imagining, as he said later, the granite wall coming through the windscreen. We crept lower and lower with my sphincter becoming tighter and tighter. We went through five hundred feet, three, two, and suddenly there was dark forbidding water ahead of us. Al shouted, "There it is!" and pointed out to our left. There, above us, was a small town with little coloured dots on the slopes above it. The dots were the local population enjoying their regular Saturday pastime of skiing. I turned steeply towards the town, just above the water, and made out the short, snow covered runway between the town and us. It was very close so I crossed the end of the runway so as to turn to the left as I curved in to it and thereby be able to keep it in sight all the way to touch down. We landed with great relief and made our way through the swirling snow to the little terminal building. The charges for fuel and landing fees were extortionate but I paid them gladly.

The rest of the journey was an anti-climax. We landed at Manchester airport (it was late at night and Woodford was closed) on January the fifteenth and I was back at my desk the next morning. My Managing Director was not pleased. I had been away for over two weeks and he wanted to know why I had done the ferry trip myself and not sent someone else. My excuse of having to keep in touch with all the activities of my department was not well received. The real reason, that I enjoyed it, would have been greeted with an explosion of wrath.

Running a busy department populated by bright individualists was not so different to my time at Boscombe Down. I still had to lead by example and persuasion rather than be heavy handed. I found that it was profitable to get the wives on your side as even macho, he-man test pilots (or perhaps especially M.H-M.T.Ps) were under the little woman's thumb. If their husbands were away for a month or so problems could arise at home and it was wise to keep a fatherly eye on things even though the wives, being mainly ex-service wives, were very capable and independent. Only occasionally did my usual offer of help in any way get taken up, and usually only for fairly trivial things. There was, however, one tragic case that stands out, although even that had it's lighter moments.

One day in February 1987 I had gone home a little early to change for a later function, when Tony Hawkes, who seemed to have become the harbinger of bad tidings, rang me. Our two Safety Equipment workers, Ian Fisher and Basil Davidson, had been working in New Assembly removing an ejection seat from a Buccaneer, when the seat gun had gone off and the seat had been blown into Basil's chest as he sat astride the aircraft's spine to guide it out. Tony told me that Bas had been taken to Stockport hospital and his condition was serious. I said that I would go to Bas's house and tell his wife. Tricia offered to come with me and, as we had done several times in the RAF, we set off together to break bad news to yet another wife. We drove to Stockport where Bas and Jan Davidson and their two daughters lived. We had never met Jan and it took some time to find their house and the corner shop that they ran. Eventually we ran it to earth and broke the news to Jan over the counter. She shut the shop and we took her to the hospital. On the way she asked very anxiously whether it was serious and I truthfully could not say, but she had been a nurse until quite recently and this gave her some feeling for the situation. Basil was dead before we arrived and Jan was inconsolable, but she was surrounded by old friends on the staff and we slipped away promising to see her as soon as possible. I dropped Trish off at home and returned to Woodford where a meeting had been convened in the Boardroom to start the investigations.

I went to see Jan the next day and offered all the help that we could give. She and her two lovely daughters were very strong and positive and we became good friends over the next few months as the business dragged on. Jan asked me to be her escort at the funeral and to read the lesson at the service, which I was very pleased to do. At the family lunch afterwards in a local hotel a formidable lady who seemed to have her own priest in tow buttonholed me. She was Bas' aunt and she immediately stated that Bas had always wanted his ashes to be scattered in Glen Coe and she was looking to me to make the arrangements! What could I say? I promised to do so. The weeks passed as the Health and Safety investigation rumbled on and the inquest took place. It was inconclusive and I concentrated on seeing that Jan and the girls were alright, I had almost forgotten about my promise until, visiting Jan in July, she told me that the family would be very grateful if I could carry it out.

My first action when I got back to the office was to get out a road atlas and find where Glen Coe was. My idea was to fly up to the British Aerospace factory at Prestwick, borrow a car and drive up to the Glen. I rang Ian Conradi, my opposite number there, to discuss the matter and we then hatched up a plot to go to the Glen by helicopter. Ian knew the CO of the Royal Navy Sea King Flight on the airfield and promised to have a word with him. The Navy was, as usual, very co-operative and not only agreed to provide a helicopter but also a Roman Catholic Padre for the occasion. So on the 30th of July I collected Bas' ashes from the undertaker and drove north through absolutely foul weather, arriving there just before lunch. I would have been earlier if I could have conjured up an aircraft but none was available. I met the Senior Pilot who introduced me to Lt Sargenson and his crew and to Father Wilson. The Padre and I were carefully briefed and climbed into bright orange survival suits, mine over my dark, funeral type suit (which never recovered) and were ushered into the Sea King.

As we flew north over the Firth of Clyde, the weather grew steadily worse and we had to fly lower and lower, until we were only 50ft above the grey, choppy sea. It was obvious that we could not go direct over the Grampian hills but the crew thought that we might be able to go the sea route and creep up the Firth of Lorn and Loch Levan to get there. But first we had to get across the Mull of Kintyre, whose tops were lost in clouds that looked very uninviting. We flew up Loch Fyne until we came to the small Loch that leads to the Crinan Canal where we were only just able to get over the bridge at it's mouth and fly down the canal until we reached the Sound of Jura at the other end. After another 45 minutes we reached the entrance to Glen Coe, where it became plain that we would never make it up the Glen to the mountains. The crew asked my opinion and I reasoned that Basil would have been pleased to know that we had tried so hard and that he would have settled for the lower reaches of the Glen. So, with a lone, startled motorist looking on from the road a mile off to the side, the Sea King landed on the pebbled riverbed. The Padre and I climbed stiffly out in our all-enveloping day-glo suits; me clutching a small green cardboard box and he his Bible and folded stole. The helicopter backed off and left us in peace in the drizzling rain. There was something faintly ridiculous but poignant about two middle aged men dressed in ill fitting orange rubber suits with bowed heads as the Padre read out the burial service and I allowed Bas' ashes to blow out in the wind. Luckily, the helicopter was able to get back into the glen and pick us up. The crew let me fly the Sea King home so at least I could put another type in my logbook.

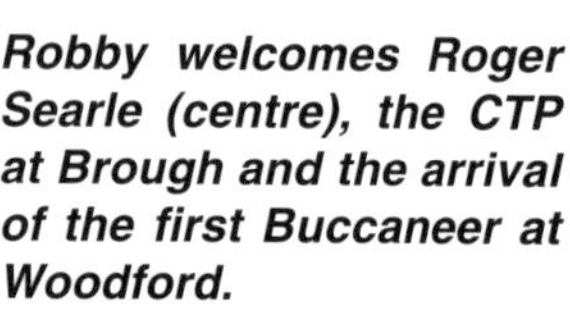

Robby welcomes Roger Searle (centre), the CTP at Brough and the arrival of the first Buccaneer at Woodford.

Running any department in a large company is a busy, ulcer-producing task. Like other department heads, the Chief Test Pilot has responsibility for the efficiency of his own part of ship and must answer to his masters for this. Luckily, test flying is a mystery to most of his masters and so the CTP is not often asked for details of his stewardship, merely hung if he gets it wrong. Of course, at the same time he has to play his full part as a test pilot, as though the Production Director had to man a lathe several times a week. This gives the CTP the advantage of being able to be familiar with the workforce without being taken advantage of. If I called a fitter an idiot he would almost certainly grin foolishly and say to his fellows, "That Robby, he's a case". If the Works Manager tried that they would down tools. I learnt my management techniques in the air force and I still maintain that the services know more about man-management than any industry. I was forced to attend several seminars on such matters in my time at Woodford, run by management consultants who, in my opinion, were earning a fortune for teaching a few self-evident truths. They were fond of saying that management could be taught. I am convinced that this is not true, or not completely. A good manager is one by nature and by experience. Choose your men carefully and you will get the leaders you need.

Well, I have got that off my chest. You may have detected that I believe in that dirty word "leadership". I do, devoutly. I tried to be a leader at Woodford, especially in the difficult times, such as during the Falklands war and the hard grind of getting the ATP into the air. I resisted any efforts by others, such as Human Resources (re-christened 'Human Remains') to interfere with "my people" and frequently used a phrase learnt in a strip club in Washington.

Bill Gevaux, an old student of mine, joined us for a brief period in 1982/83. He is an ebullient, larger than life character who has lead me astray many times. He and I had completed a 748 sales tour of South America, yet again, and were recuperating in Washington for a few days. We had taken to frequenting a strip club called 'The Cat Mieow' because the beer was cheaper there (honestly). I sat sipping a Budweiser at the bar as one of the girls went through her routine on the small stage. As she reached her denouement the small door behind her opened and on came Bill and Race Pilbrow the engineer. They both had knotted handkerchiefs on their heads, their trousers rolled up and more hankies in each hand. They proceeded to do a Morris dance to the inappropriate tune of 'The Stripper'. The girl stood stark naked, hands on hips and watched them. They earned more applause than she had and, finally, she could take no more.

"Get off." She shouted, "You're ruining my Goddamned act!"

A good phrase to use in times of stress I have found.

Chapter Six

Testing Times

Although I seem to have given the impression that the test pilot's life consists of going on jollies around the world, he actually does this only on a fill in basis. His main task is to live up to his title and test aircraft. There are several kinds of test pilot; those in the services engage in research and acceptance testing at DERA Boscombe Down. Industry pilots do some research testing of aircraft and equipment and production testing of aircraft fresh off the line but their main purpose in life is the development testing of prototype aircraft from first flight to entry into service. Nearly all aircraft company sites specialise in either military or civil aircraft. Woodford in my time was unique in being split 50-50 between military and civil aircraft production. The requirements of the two types of customer were markedly different, as were the requirements of the two acceptance organisations, Boscombe Down and the CAA. In the case of Boscombe Down, performance and handling qualities are paramount, whilst the CAA, on behalf of the civil customer, insists on safety considerations. The civil authority does not care if an aircraft can only carry one passenger from Woodford to Manchester Airport, ten miles or so, as long as it is done safely. Performance in the civil world is the province of the customer airline and competition takes care of that. The test pilots at Woodford had to be fluent in both testing philosophies.

When I joined Woodford I was fully immersed in the military ethic and my first tasks were concerned with military aircraft. Indeed the main reason that the RAF released me was so that I could carry the military view through into the testing of the proposed AEW Nimrod. At the time of my joining some preliminary testing of the prototype AEW radar had started in a converted Comet 4c, XW626, known as the Comrod. I flew some of the

Comet 4C XW626 was heavily modified to carry the planned AEW nose radar, which was to be later fitted to the Nimrod AEW3.

radar tests in 1978 and was co-pilot to Charles Masefield for the aircraft's display at Farnborough that year. (It was memorable only because I had caught some dreadful lurgy of the feet in Trinidad and had to fly in carpet slippers at the show to cover my poor swollen feet).

By the beginning of 1979, the initial radar trials on XW626 were coming to an end and the Ministry decided to reclaim the aircraft and use it for general equipment trials at RAE Bedford. XW626 had been modified for the radar trials by putting a large radome on the nose, without the balancing tail radome due to go on the production aircraft. This meant that it's directional stability was reduced, rather like a dart with extra flights on the point. This had been fairly unimportant during our mundane radar tests when the aircraft had been flown exclusively by company test pilots but handing over to the RAE was another story. It would need some sort of official clearance and this would entail some basic handling tests to establish the flight envelope, albeit a very restricted one. I was given this job and the first tests were to be the rolling characteristics. This seemed to be a simple enough task.

On April the 23rd, Dave Pearson and I briefed to carry out the first handling flight. I queried whether the rolls were to be with or without rudder assistance and received a woolly sort of an answer from the Flight Test department. I gathered that it was rather up to me. It would be preferable if it could meet the requirements without rudder but if I had to I could use it. The first part of the flight was without incident. Rolls with restricted aileron deflection were fine and we were ready to move on to rolls with full aileron. It should be explained that every aircraft has a sideslip angle limit over which the fin is likely to snap off (like on an early Victor) or at least become very over stressed. XW626 had a limit of 17 degrees at low speed and I was very conscious of this.

I put on 45 degrees of left bank and, when the speed and attitude were correct, I rapidly applied full right aileron, holding the wheel hard on the stop and watching the sideslip gauge like a hawk. The aircraft started to roll quite nicely but then paused, the nose tucked down a little and the sideslip accelerated so swiftly that I was unable to control it with rudder. It left the 17 degree limit far behind and the needle went off the stops at something over 28 degrees before I could get the poor beast back under control. You could almost feel the fuselage bending and hear the fin groaning with the strain. It was a most uncomfortable manoeuvre that left our hearts in our mouths. I cancelled the rest of the sortie and flew home as stress free as possible, very aware that the fin might depart at any moment.

The debriefing was quite heated. Why was this not foreseen? Whose fault was it? What could we do about it? - What we actually did was nothing, except for a very thorough stress check. We continued the tests and eventually the RAE was persuaded to accept the aircraft as it was, with very restrictive limitations as to the amount of aileron that could be used. XW626 went on to do many years of valiant service after that and was eventually broken up for scrap.

Overleaf: de Havilland Comet 4C XW626 arriving at Farnborough in 1978 with Robby and Sir Charles Masefield at the controls.

BRITISH AEROSPACE - WOODFORD

The Nimrod MR (Maritime Reconnaissance) had been in service for many years, first as the MR.1 and then, after a major equipment refit, as the MR.2. In 1979, the MOD decided to add ECM (Electronic Counter Measures) to the aircraft and wing tip pods were designed to accommodate it. These were very large tubular structures set at a slight nose down angle to give minimum drag at patrol speeds. The preliminary handling tests in this configuration on XV241 showed no problems and Tony Hawkes, who was then the project pilot, began the stalling tests. Up until then, the Nimrod had very benign stalling characteristics so Tony did not expect any problems. However, at the beginning of March 1980 he flew a sortie on which he was to carry out the first fully developed stalls. The aircraft returned to Woodford much earlier than expected and Charles Masefield and I sat in on the debriefing. Apparently, Tony had carried out the

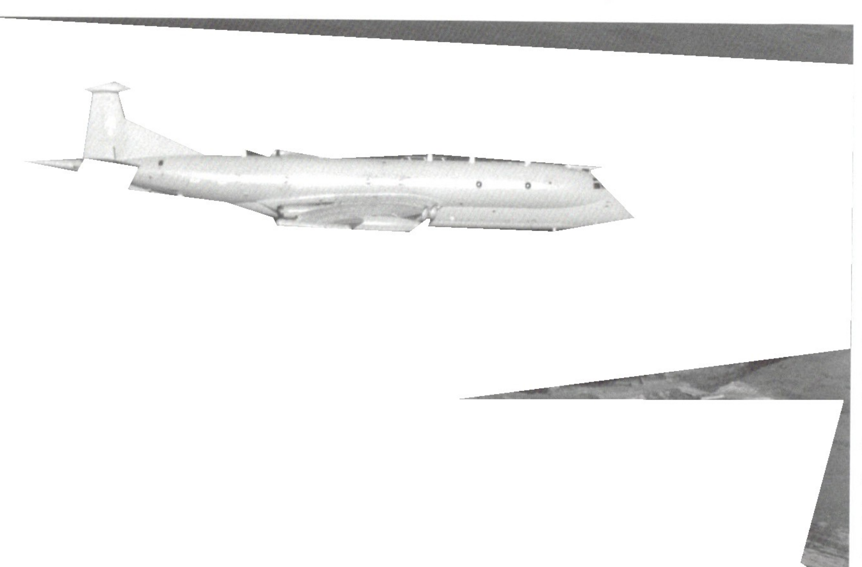

Nimrod MR.2 XV241 was the first of its type to be fitted with ECM wing tip pods. (Crown Copyright).

preliminary approaches to the stall with no mishaps but, as he reduced speed down to where he expected the first signs of pre-stall buffet, the nose of the aircraft suddenly yawed off to the right and the aircraft rolled right into a 60-degree bank. After recovering from this unexpected and alarming excursion he very wisely and properly discontinued the tests and returned home to report on the phenomena. Test pilots are paid to take risks but also to be cautious, especially with very valuable aircraft.

The radical change in the stall caused a lot of head scratching and it was obvious that this was unacceptable for service use. It was felt however that any fixes to overcome the problem could not be formulated until the true stalling characteristics beyond the nose slice were known. Therefore we would try to fight our way through the critical speed band and attempt to reach the stalling speeds previously cleared on the pod-less Nimrod. The next day, Charles and I took off and climbed to 10,000 feet over Lincolnshire to repeat the tests. Charles throttled back the engines and carefully trimmed the aircraft at the assigned flaps up trim speed. He then began to reduce speed at a steady one knot per second decrement until the first mild buffet was felt. As the speed was reduced below this the handling felt normal with all controls effective but at five knots above the expected stalling speed, the nose sliced violently to the right and the starboard wing dropped quickly to some 60 degrees. At least we had reproduced the phenomena and had it all on tape. We talked about it and decided that it should be possible to use the rudders coarsely to get through the yaw. Charles very generously invited me to try this. I repeated the procedure until, as the nose sliced right, I quickly put on full left rudder and continued pulling. By judiciously using rudder to minimise the yawing I managed to reach the stall proper when the nose dropped. However, at the same time, the right wing dropped sharply until we were in a most uncomfortable attitude and had lost several thousand feet before recovering. We repeated this several times with different flap and engine settings and with all the data in the can we returned home.

Now began a series of wind tunnel tests on a large Nimrod model fitted with pods. The low speed wind tunnel was just downstairs from our offices (as was obvious from the noise) which made it very convenient to drop in and observe the runs. The aerodynamicists tried various attachments to keep the airflow smooth at the critical angle of attack that we had found and eventually settled for a line of vortex generators on the upper wing surfaces just inboard of the pods. Vortex generators (VGs) are plates set at an angle to the airflow to produce small vortices that regenerate the boundary layer air and delay it's separation from the wing surface; this separation is what causes a stall. This approach showed promise and a series of VGs were stuck onto the aircraft's wings. The idea was that we would start the tests with too many VGs and after each flight we would take one off each wing until we reached the most efficient number. Perhaps we would now run a computer programme to replace all these trials but such programmes did not exist then.

It was the beginning of May before we were ready to re-commence the trials and on the 9th of May, Tony Hawkes and I flew the first flight with VGs fitted to repeat the tests. We found that they modified the effects and, although the nose slice was still apparent, we reckoned that it was now acceptable and that Boscombe Down would agree with us (we hoped). The stall was still marked by a pronounced wing drop, but this could be held by the ailerons alone and at least it was at the designed stalling speed. Boscombe Down was invited to come and look at the stall and eventually agreed that it was acceptable. However, the debate was to rumble on for several years and would resurface with the Nimrod AEW.

Meanwhile we got on with refining the number of VGs on each wing. Before each electronic equipment test flight we would take off a pair of VGs and, at the end of the flight, carry out a full suite of stalls. Not a popular exercise with the avionics department men aboard who were used to fairly sedate flights. We worked our way down from 26 each side to 17. Each VG was stuck on with double-sided tape so that it would be easy to remove; too easy. On the final test flight with the definitive number on the wings we checked the characteristics and agreed that we had achieved the best compromise possible. After landing it was found that some of our VGs had removed themselves. We had 15 on one side and 13 on the other. We did not have the cheek to call that the final solution so put back the missing VGs and had them riveted on.

One of the differences between military and civil testing is the concentration, in the latter case, on specific minimum safely speeds. During a take off in a multi-engined aircraft there is a speed at which, in the event of an engine failure, it is safe to continue. Below this speed, directional control cannot be maintained and the take off must be aborted. This speed is called V1. There is a similar minimum speed on the approach to land below which control cannot be maintained if it is necessary to abort the landing. Someone has to establish these speeds and so the test pilot has to carry out engine cuts at various reducing speeds until he finds one below which he loses control. This speed is called VMCA (minimum control speed in the air). A small factor is added to this speed to allow for average pilot ability and other imponderables so as to establish V1. There are of course many other minimum speeds to find but VMCA is the one that causes the most debate between the manufacturer and the certificating authority.

In 1964, when I was the Senior Pilot on E Squadron at Boscombe Down, I was given the task of accepting the HS.748 for the Queen's Flight. I found it to be a delightful aircraft but I could never quite reproduce the VMCA that Jimmy Harrison (the then Chief Test Pilot at Woodford) had managed to get past the CAA. I was always two knots higher. However it was a fairly esoteric disagreement and at V1 the aircraft was perfectly safe. In 1969, I was a tutor at ETPS and I had to teach asymmetric (engine out) testing. I carried out hundreds of engine cuts on various aircraft, in particular on the Andover C.1, the military version of the HS.748. Again I could never get down to the company VMCA. In 1984 I found myself in Jimmy Harrison's position, arguing with the CAA that the HS.748 series 2B, with more powerful engines, still met the original VMCA. Gamekeeper turned poacher? Luckily, Jimmy's silky words were as persuasive as ever and the speeds were accepted. But only after several hours in the air spent in quite critical situations.

Andover CC.2 XS789 wa delivered to the Queer Flight in July 1964. (via RCS

Let me give you a flavour of a typical VMCA test. The aircraft is first loaded to give an extreme aft centre of gravity, to ensure the minimum directional stability. Very little fuel is carried so that the aircraft is light enough to avoid reaching stalling speed before VMCA. The tests are to be carried out at very low level so that engine power is the same as at take off. So you cannot go too far away from base because you are short of fuel, but you need to go to an area of smooth air, preferably over the sea, so that you can legally fly below 1,000 ft. This is not an easy equation to solve. You have very little time to spend on actual testing and you have to pick a day when the weather is unusually good, especially for the north west of England.

Let us suppose that all this comes together and the aircraft is serviceable on the day. You fly to the chosen area, settle the aircraft just above the sea, set all trimmers to take off position, select take off flap and slow down to a speed some five knots below the test speed. You now put full power on both engines and get your head down to concentrate on holding the exact test speed in the ensuing steep climb. As soon as you are ready, and not above 1,000 ft, you call cut and your co-pilot switches off the fuel to the critical engine to reproduce a failure. You now have to pause for one second, to allow for pilot recognition of the failure. During this pause, the aircraft yaws away from your remaining engine and rolls inexorably in the same direction. Also during this time you are supposed to observe that the sideslip limit is not exceeded and that no dangerous attitudes are reached. After that long, long second passes you take control, putting on opposite rudder (using not more than the allowed foot force) and opposite aileron to level the wings; all the time trying to hold to the exact knot that elusive speed. If all is well, you try again and again at slightly reducing speeds until you reach a speed where you cannot regain control without reducing power on the live engine. At that speed you cannot afford to wait that one second and the sea sometimes gets awfully close. With all that in the can you hurry home with an anxious eye on the rapidly reducing fuel. All that is left is to debrief the members of the design team who are seldom pleased with your results and mutter things like, "Well, Jimmy Harrison used to do it!"

I thought that I had given up gliding when I left ETPS. BAe had other ideas. It had long been obvious that the high level of internal noise in turbo-prop aircraft was one of the reasons that passengers preferred jets. A study was begun at Woodford in 1982 to try to alleviate this. To analyse the causes of the excessive noise we needed to separate the engine noise from that of the air rushing over the airframe. The only way to do this, the engineers said, was to fly with all the engines shut down and record the noise levels at various speeds. Simple! Off you go Robinson. I set out to minimise the obvious risks by careful preparation.

My first priority was to try to ensure that when I wanted to re-start the engines they would indeed re-start. I therefore ordered an extra battery to be fitted. My next priority was to give myself some confidence that if the engines would not re-start I could glide the aircraft to a successful landing. To do this I would need an airfield with good long range RADAR and with Air Traffic controllers with experience of guiding engine-out aircraft to dead stick landings. We would also need a good long runway. Boscombe Down fulfilled all my requirements and so I contacted my old friends there and it was arranged.

As is so often the case in test flying, we now came up against time and weather. The aircraft, a new series 2B, would not be available after the 6th August when it would have to have the recording equipment removed and be fitted out to go to Farnborough for the SBAC show on the 4th of September. Ideally, we ought to have a cloud base of 2,000 feet at Boscombe to allow us to land there if necessary. For three days Dick Muir and I waited for the weather to relent. Finally, on the 6th, I rang Boscombe and was told that the cloud base was still a foggy 800 feet. There was nothing for it, we had to go and rely on the controller's expertise if the worst happened. Of course our radios must work, but we had two so that was all right.

On the way down to Wiltshire we climbed to our starting height of 20,000 feet and contacted Boscombe tower. When all was ready I asked Dick to feather both engines. It went really quiet; quieter than we had intended, for both radios failed! We had found a design fault that had been lying in wait for years. When both generators failed, which of course they did with no engines to drive them, the radios lost all electrical power. We were by now in cloud, blind as well as deaf and dumb. At least the emergency instruments worked. Having gone this far we might as well get some results so I held my speed until the recording was complete and, with my fingers crossed, asked Dick to restart the engines. He unfeathered the left-hand engine and switched on the relight switches. It started like a charm, as did the other engine. We breathed again. I started to climb back up to the clear blue sky above the clouds and called Boscombe on our now functioning radio to explain our strange silence. Now we considered our next move. I rationalized that if the engines had re-lit once they would do it again. We would press on. We did another twelve engineless glides before turning for home. I would like to think that we made a difference but I don't think we did. Turbo-props are still noisy.

Chapter Seven

The Military Side

Woodford had long been known for it's military aircraft. The Lancaster is of course legendary, as is the Anson and, in more recent times, the Vulcan. When I arrived at Woodford in 1978 we were just completing the conversion of the Victor 2s to the tanker role (I was able to take part in the delivery of the last two aircraft) and we were deep in the modification programme to convert the Nimrod MR.1s to MR.2s. The Nimrod AEW.3 was yet to fly but we were trying hard to sell a military version of the 748 to anyone who would listen. The RAF already used the 748 in the Queen's Flight and a rear-loading version, the Andover C.1, was proving it's worth in the short-range freight and parachuting role. However, we had for some time been trying to interest the Air Staff in a maritime version with a largish radome underneath, the Coastguarder. As an old Air Staff man I really believed in this aircraft. It was tailor made for the inshore fisheries protection and oilrig patrol roles, thereby releasing the Nimrods for their proper role of long-range patrol, the RAF was being it's usual obstinate self and did not want to know. So I hatched a plot.

I had got wind of an event called Sea Search 81, a maritime reconnaissance competition being held as part of the 1981 Greenham Common Air Show. The competitors were coming from all over the world, all of them military, flying the latest versions of maritime aircraft such as the Lockheed P-3 Orion of the US Navy, the Breguet Atlantique of the French Navy and, of course, the RAF Nimrod. I contacted the organizers and they sent me an entry form, which I duly filled in and sent off, telling nobody else in the company. My entry was accepted with alacrity and I now had to come clean and tell my bosses what I had done. The MD, Norman Barber, was quite amenable, possibly not quite realising what was involved, however, the sales Director was not so convinced, after all he owned the aircraft and his budget would have to cover the costs. I eventually convinced him that it would give the Coastguarder good exposure and could not embarrass the company by beating our other product, the Nimrod, another of his worries.

My next task was to pick the crew. The obvious choice for Captain was Harry Fisher who had been a Coastal Command Shackleton pilot before joining Woodford.

G-BDVH in the guise of the 'Coastguarder'. (Harry Holmes).

However, Harry was a big and very forceful man and I wanted Reg Castle, our senior navigator, to have free reign as the tactical leader. So I braved Harry's wrath and picked Kevin Moorhouse, an excellent pilot who had recently graduated to the left-hand seat of the 748. He was a much gentler soul than "Big H" but still an excellent Captain. As his co-pilot I chose Dick Muir, an ex-flight test observer and Ted Hartley, one of our Flight Engineers, as an observer. As one of the competition categories was for the best ship photography, I persuaded Fred Hill, our expert company photographer, to join us. We needed one other crewmember, an extra observer to help with the visual search. Part of the competition was a ship identification test and I had no one in the department who claimed to be any good at that. However, I knew of an engineer in the Customer Support department, Peter Petherbridge, who was not aircrew but was an Air Training Corps Officer and who was a whiz at aircraft recognition. I reasoned, with very little to back it up, that he would have the right sort of mind to study ship silhouettes and ultimately be a whiz at ship recognition as well. He was mad keen to take part. The party was completed by the addition of John Dixon, a customer support engineer, who would keep the aircraft flying throughout the week. I believe he also managed to fly quite a bit as an extra observer.

I waved off my gallant crew and to a large extent forgot about them as I got on with the every day tasks. On the evening of the competition day my home telephone rang, it was Kevin.

The winner of the 'Sea Search 81' competition held at Greenham Common was HS.748 'Coastguarder' G-BCDZ. Sadly, the RAF was focussed on increasing it's Nimrod fleet, rather than purchasing the useful Coastguarder. (Harry Holmes).

"Hi Kevin. How did it go?" I said, not expecting anything more than "Not too bad".

"Well," he said rather diffidently "I'm sorry to say," he paused long enough to give me palpitations, "we won every category except that of the furthest travelled contestant, a New Zealand crew won that."

You can imagine my feelings. Our little aircraft with a scratch civilian crew had beaten all the professionals. This should put the Coastguarder on the map.

The next morning I flew the company Dove down to Greenham Common to congratulate the crew and to observe the presentation ceremony. The only black moment was when Ken Edgerton, our head salesman, came up to me and said "Don't ever do that to me again" and he meant it. He had not expected us to win and had made no publicity preparation. Of course the RAF never bought the Coastguarder, they were too interested in getting approval for extra Nimrods.

Since July 1980, we had been carrying out a series of tests of the AEW (Airborne Early Warning) version of the Nimrod. Johnny Cruse was the Project Pilot and had kept nearly all of the handling testing to himself. In February 1981, when I had been CTP for all of ten days, I decided that it was time that I flew it as Captain. The scheduled tests were a series of high-speed runs at altitude, the first time that the aircraft would be flown at its maximum design Mach number of 0.82. So, with Johnny as my co-pilot, I climbed the aircraft, XV286, to 30,000 feet and settled it down at the required initial Mach number, 0.80. After the requisite recordings were made we accelerated to the next increment and so on until we reached the limit of 0.82 Mach. At this speed we were well into compressibility buffet and the airflow over the flight-refuelling probe on the cabin roof made it very noisy. I found that to keep the speed constant I was having to edge the throttles forward until I could no longer maintain the speed. I looked for a reason and immediately found it. The Jet Pipe Temperatures in the two inboard engines were right off the clock; in fact it was difficult to see if there were any needles on the gauges as they were so far to the right. I hastily throttled the two engines back but the JPTs obstinately remained in the red. I told Johnny to cut off the fuel to those engines and saw with some relief that the temperatures reduced to near ambient. We had obviously suffered a double engine compressor stall, a most unusual occurrence. I consulted the Flight engineer, Bob Pogson, but he had no explanation so we tried to relight number two. As soon as Johnny opened the high-pressure cock to feed fuel to the burners the JPT soared to it's previous record value. He hastily shut it down. We would have to limp home on two.

It was a fairly nervous homecoming as, if you lose two engines, what is there to say that you might not lose another, or perhaps two more? We did not put out an emergency call as the project was at a very sensitive juncture and any listening aircraft spotter would soon pass on the fact that the AEW project was in trouble to a gleeful press. So we crept into Woodford off a direct approach merely telling ATC that we needed to be met by the fire service and to inform the Technical Director, John Scott-Wilson.

Overleaf: Nimrod AEW.3 XV286 on it's maiden flight with Sir Charles Masefield and Johnny Cruse at the controls. This photograph was taken from '147', being flown by Robby and Peter Henley.

After landing and shutting down, Johnny, Bob and I peered into the tail pipes of number's two and three engines. With the aid of a torch we could make out that there was very little left of the turbines and the pipes themselves bore evidence of extremely high temperatures. As Johnny and I walked away from the aircraft we were intercepted by John Scott-Wilson. He, of course, was only interested in the reason for our asking for him to be at the debriefing. We, on the other hand, were a little hyper at having got safely home after a fairly anxious time.

Robby and Bill Gevaux bring XZ281 close to the camera aircraft on the 24th November 1982. This aircraft was eventually scrapped at Abingdon in 1991.

"Hello John. I don't think Johnny is going to let me fly his baby again." I quipped. John wrinkled his high domed brow. He saw nothing to be flippant about and we went in to the debriefing in brooding silence. The room was packed. Everyone with any interest in the project had crowded in, luckily leaving two free seats for the two suspects at the end of the long table. It felt more like a trial than a debriefing. As usual all those with vested interests such as the designers and the engine men were convinced, or hoped, that we pilots were responsible. Guilty until proven innocent is the rule. We insisted that we had not mishandled the throttles as the prosecution maintained. There was some unusual effect at play here and it would be no use arguing until the instrumentation tapes were read. One point of interest was that the flight observers had heard a very loud explosion at the time of the incident but had thought that as it was so loud we on the flight deck must have heard it, so they had said nothing! The meeting broke up with nothing resolved.

It took several days for the tapes to become available and for the meeting to be reconvened. The traces were laid out on the table and I asked for the record of the throttle positions to be identified. This proved beyond all doubt that we had not been cavalier with their handling. Indeed we had only advanced them by one eighth of an inch and all four had been advanced together. Therefore there was some unexplained phenomenon affecting only the inboard engines. Almost certainly it had to be aerodynamic. Bill James, the head aerodynamicist, suggested a wind tunnel programme of tests and these were undertaken as a matter of extreme urgency as, even after the fitting of two new engines, we could not fly until the problem was solved. Of course we now had two other players in the act, the engine makers Rolls Royce and the Ministry of Defence, who owned the aircraft. Apart from banging our gums nobody could make any progress until we had the results of the wind tunnel tests.

Wind tunnel testing is a slow business but with all the pressure on the project overtime was no object and within two days I was able to see the results. In fact I could literally see them as a smoke visualization technique was being used and at a scale speed of 0.82 Mach one could see a high-energy vortex entering the inboard intake. The vortex was being formed at the intersection of the old Nimrod nose with the new large nose radome. All was explained. Two VG's just in front of the windscreens solved the problem.

XZ285 was one of three aircraft that served with the Joint Trials Unit before being broken up for spares in 1992.

The Boeing AWACs had a very large radome on a tripod on top of the fuselage. It looked ugly and added significant drag as well as having the slight disadvantage of the nose, tail and wing tips of the aircraft getting in the way of the radar beam when looking down. The Marconi solution to where to put the radar dome was ingenious in the extreme. There were to be two radomes, one looking forward on the nose and one looking rearward on the tail. The plan was for one radar scanner to sweep through 180 degrees and, when it completed it's sweep, the other scanner would take up the scan and complete the 360 degrees. The two resulting radar pictures were to be combined on one screen in the cabin, thus in effect making the AEW aircraft disappear. When we eventually tried it out in the air the system worked very well although there were some development problems. For instance there was the "banana effect" as we named it. In the air the lift generated by the wings and the down force on the tailplane combined to give the fuselage a slight bend, this varied with speed. This of course made the radar returns from the two scanners slightly out of synchronization and gave false information about any target. However modern digital electronics are wonderful and the solution lay in a small change in the software.

This view of XZ286 clearly displays the two large radomes unique to the AEW.3.

We began electronic development trials in 1981 whilst still continuing to carry out the handling trials. BAe was responsible for the airframe and Marconi for the electronic suite so we provided the pilots, flight engineer and navigator and they crewed the rear of the aircraft. This produced a few tensions in the early days as none of the Marconi engineers were aircrew trained, had no idea of intercom discipline and had to be trained in all aspects of survival. However, we quickly settled down as an integrated trials team only occasionally giving me heart attacks by the use of computer jargon, such as "It's crashed!" The sorties were long, up to 10 hours, and very boring for the front crew, although the Marconi men were working their socks off down the back. Most of the sorties involved RAF fighter aircraft carrying out various manoeuvres to provide targets to test the equipment. Luckily, making the arrangements for the target aircraft was a Marconi responsibility as that was very time consuming.

Let me set out a typical trials day. The briefing involving some 30 people started at nine o'clock in the morning with the Captain of the aircraft in the chair. The Marconi team would have already held their own briefing, probably the night before. After the main briefing the front crew would file a flight plan and, most important of all, collect the rations from Doreen, the mess manageress. Woe betide anyone who forgot the rations. 10 hours with no food and drink would have reduced the crew to mutiny. The rear crew meanwhile went out to the aircraft for an hour's preliminary tests and to warm up the kit. The Flight Engineer would at this time be aboard to do his pre-flight checks and to run the electrical power for the ground tests. An hour before the scheduled take off time the pilots and navigator would deign to take their seats and begin the final checks leading to starting the engines and, when all was ready, taxyng to the take off point. Now came the easy bit, the take off and climb to our operating area, usually over Lincolnshire and the North Sea, and setting up a race track pattern at our trials height, about 25,000 feet. The autopilot was programmed to maintain the pattern so the only high spot of the next few hours was eating our rations and drinking endless cups of coffee. To relieve my boredom I would wander down the back to watch the trials team at work. Over the next five years I observed the system gradually improving until it became reliable and seemed, to my layman's eye, to do it's job. There were others who had different ideas.

In 1985 a team of RAF specialists joined us. Their task was to assess the system and report on it's progress to their masters. I think perhaps that their masters had a separate agenda. The members of the team were nice blokes, entering into the social side of the company with enthusiasm, becoming regular attendees at our Lancaster Club and giving their own parties at the house they had rented in Stockport. They were all aircrew so they integrated with the trials team very easily. They gave us no problems although I think that the Marconi men began to feel uneasy. It must have been difficult to carry out development tests with someone looking over their shoulders and reporting every little hitch (which are inevitable in any trials) to higher-ups who were intent on seeing the system fail. As time went by it became obvious that the project was in trouble politically and it culminated with a flight on the 18th November 1986.

I was told that the Secretary of State for Defence, Mr George Younger, was coming to fly with us to see how things were going. It was obvious that this was a political visit, not idle curiosity. Mr. Younger could not be expected to understand the technical aspects of the system and his presence, I surmised, was so that he could say truthfully that he had observed it in action before making a decision on it's viability. I met Mr. Younger at the briefing, took him aboard and sat him on the jump seat behind me. He was extremely pleasant, taking a great interest in our preparations for flight but keeping out of the way. The take off and climb went without a hitch and when we reached our patrol station the Squadron Leader in charge of the RAF team led him back to observe the demonstration. I am not sure that the RAF men ever knew that I could listen in to their private intercom but I could and I heard them talking to the Minister and subtly denigrating the performance of the system with remarks such as "You see, Sir, there is the problem we spoke about." Eventually the demonstration was over and Mr. Younger came back to the flight deck and we returned to base where, after landing, I presented him with a company AEW tie. He changed from his borrowed flying suit, climbed into his car and left. He did not attend the debriefing, neither did the RAF team. The next week it was announced that the project was cancelled and that the Air Force would be getting the AWACS that it had wanted all along.

Although we were sorry that the project had been cancelled, we of BAe were not too upset. It is never nice to be associated with a failure but we had delivered, on schedule, all six airframes to RAF Waddington where they were to be fitted out with the Marconi electronics. So we had been paid our money. It was a different case for Marconi.

Overleaf: Excellent air to air of XV286 during one of it's early flights. (Ian Lowe).

XZ286

Throughout the eighties we still persisted in marketing the 748. One of our efforts was in Iraq. In April 1982 I flew a 748 to Baghdad with a large team of engineers from Marconi and BAe onboard. It was a rather nervous flight as Iraq was at war and we had to fly at night with no lights on and in radio silence. The main object of our visit was to sell Nimrod AEWs to the Iraqi Airforce. Of course in 1982 Iraq was at war with Iran and Saddam Hussein was one of the good guys. The Gulf States were trying to put together a regional defence system and the final choice of AEW would be mainly paid for with Saudi Arabian money. It all seems a most unlikely exercise now but at the time it promised to be a very big deal.

We spent a week talking to General Raschid, the Chief of the Iraqi Air Force, and his staff and I was most impressed with the quality of himself and his officers. All had PhDs from western Universities and were experts in their field. They gave us a hard time during the day but went a bit wild in the evenings. Their capacity for Chivas Regal whiskey was outstanding, as was their appetite for roast lamb eaten with the hands. They did not press us to sheep's eyes though. They were extremely civil and urbane. On one of the hospitality tours I found myself sitting in a black Bedouin goats hair tent next to a young Lieutenant Colonel. For something to say I asked him what sort of wood was used for the tent's framework. "My dear chap" he said in Oxford English, "I have no bloody idea."

One day, whilst for once the talks went on without me, I carried out a demonstration of the 748 to an Airforce Colonel and his number two. The Colonel was the typically incisive Iraqi officer that I had by now come to expect. His number two however was totally subservient to his boss and was never allowed to touch the controls. The Colonel would not tell me where we were going, although I found out later that we had been to a desert strip called Baqoubah. I, not speaking any Arabic, was relieved when the Colonel said that he would do all the radio work. We flew up country, he doing all the flying whilst talking up a storm on the R/T. Eventually we reached a small desert strip with, I could see, gun emplacements round the perimeter. On the final approach my companion suddenly asked me to take over and show him a single engined overshoot and landing. I feathered the port engine, switched on the water methanol and opened up to full power on the other engine. It was of course a very hot day and the little plane was quite sluggish but nevertheless it coped gamely and we climbed to a thousand feet and turned downwind to land. I should at this point explain that the salesmen, in their wisdom, had insisted that we use a camouflaged aircraft for the exercise. An unwise choice as I was about to find out.

One thing that I did not know was that the Colonel had been unable to raise anyone on the radio. You can imagine the feelings of the men on the ground. Here was a strange aircraft of a type that they did not recognize, with one engine feathered and obviously of military origin, approaching their airstrip completely unannounced. Add to this that they were some five miles behind a very active front line and it was to be expected that they would react nervously. I landed and taxied off the oiled sand strip and we were immediately surrounded by Jeeps mounting large calibre machine guns and men pointing automatic rifles at me, in the cockpit. They looked scared and so did I, I expect. The

Colonel said a few well-chosen Arabic words, laughed, unstrapped and went down the back. I peered back out of my side window and saw that half of the guns were now switched to cover the rear door. I felt the door open and straightaway the situation was transformed. Guns were dropped, smiles of relief wreathed all faces and people clapped each other on their shoulders, obviously saying, "It's Colonel Thingy. He's a wag." Colonel "Thingy" said a few words of encouragement to his men and came back with a great grin on his face. I restarted the engine and got out of there as quickly as I could

  After two more days of talks we left Baghdad in the dead of night, again in radio silence and with no navigation lights; returning to Woodford via Hail, Cairo, Athens and Nice. We arrived home on the 25th of April to most unexpected news.

Chapter Eight

The Falklands Effort

The story of the Falklands war has been told many times but I have seen little about the efforts of the aviation industry supporting our forces. Many companies produced minor miracles to modify, test and supply equipment. I cannot cover all companies, I can only tell you of the efforts of BAe Manchester, of the wartime spirit that was generated and the selfless giving of time and ingenuity by all levels of the workforce, from the Managing Director to the hangar cleaners.

Whilst in Baghdad we had been totally cut off from the outside world. We were completely unaware that Argentina had invaded the Falklands and that we, the Brits, were preparing to fight back. The first news we had of the conflict was when we reached Athens on the 24th of April. Even then we only gained a sketchy picture from the Greek media so when we arrived back at Woodford on the 25th I was totally unprepared for the uncharacteristic bustle in the flight sheds.

I was met at the aircraft by Johnny Cruse who quickly filled me in. Apparently on the 14th of April the Board of Directors had received a telephone call from the Ministry of Defence asking how long it would take to give the Nimrod a flight refuelling capability. As it happened Charles Masefield and I had carried out a test in 1980 to see if such a thing could be done. We flew behind a Victor tanker and, although we had no probe fitted, we carried out a few approaches to the drogue. This had showed up some quite serious deficiencies but at least the engineers had a good idea of what would be entailed. John Scott-Wilson, the Technical Director, had replied to the Ministry man that we could do it in a month, a quite outrageously short time. Normally such a modification would take a year at least but normal procurement procedures were being thrown out the window. Time was pressing; the Task Force was already at sea and needed the protection of maritime reconnaissance. The normal combat radius of the Nimrod is some 1,000 miles if one is to have a useful patrol time. From Ascension Island, where the task force was based, to the Falklands was 3,800 miles!

Nice view of a Nimrod refuelling from a Victor tanker, two very large aircraft just a few feet apart.

XV229 fitted with the 'borrowed' Vulcan refuelling probe.

Without the cover of the Nimrods the fleet would have no knowledge of enemy surface ships or, in particular, of enemy submarines. The assault would have to wait until we delivered the modified aircraft. The first delivery was made on May the first, not a month but a mere 18 days after that phone call.

The main handling problem that the early 1980 trials had shown up was that the Nimrod's aileron/rudder interconnection, (necessary for directional stability), gave unacceptable characteristics during the approach to the drogue. As the pilot used the ailerons to line up the probe with the drogue, the interconnect moved the rudders in such a way as to yaw the aircraft a little and thus to move the probe away from the drogue. To overcome this we fitted a switch on the flight engineer's panel that he could use to cut out the interconnect when the aircraft was approaching the tanker. XV229 was fitted with a probe and the basic airframe modifications for preliminary handling tests; no piping was fitted at this juncture as it was still being designed. On the 27th of April, Johnny Cruse and Flt Lt Tony Banfield took off in 229 to test the new cut out and to try the aircraft out behind a tanker. I had decided that it was better for the Boscombe Down pilot to take the right hand seat, as he was vastly experienced in flight refuelling. However, I thought that I needed to watch the initial tests so I stood behind the seats.

As we rotated on take off it was obvious that Johnny was having big problems. The aircraft was yawing violently and rolling from side to side. The new modification must be the problem. Johnny shouted to Bob Pogson, the flight engineer, to reverse the position of the cut out switch. Now came the comical bit, at least to me, the observer. The switch had been fitted at the top of the panel. Bob was short and could only reach the switch by standing up. He unstrapped and attempted to reach the switch, however, every time he stretched out his arm the yaw of the aircraft threw him back and he missed it. This went on for some time as Johnny wrestled the aircraft round onto the downwind leg to attempt an emergency landing but eventually Bob made it and the aircraft immediately reverted to it's docile self. After landing it was found that the interconnect had been wired the wrong way round. More haste less speed! After the wiring was rectified we flew the aircraft successfully the next day, carrying out successful dry contacts with a Victor tanker.

A more refined version of the probe was later fitted to all of the RAFs Nimrods.

Overleaf: The crew of XV229 pose after the first flight of a Nimrod with a refuelling probe.

It is, I think, worthwhile describing the hasty modifications made to give the Nimrod an air-to-air refuelling capability. The first requirement was the probe. They were in short supply as the Vulcan force was also being refitted with them. However we already possessed one. In 1980 we had bought a redundant Vulcan from the air force to serve as our gate guardian. It still had it's probe. We used the probe for our tests, selling it back to the MOD for what we had paid for the whole Vulcan. Business is business. An "A" frame was fitted on the Nimrod's cabin roof, just above the pilots' heads and producing a lot of wind noise. This frame supported the probe at mid point. The rear of the probe was attached to a metal pipe that was led down through the specially modified upper escape hatch, which now became unusable. This pipe became bifurcated and descended behind the Captain's seat where it joined a pair of rubber hoses. These hoses were of the standard road tanker type as these were the only hoses available in sufficient length to allow us to lead it through the cabin with no joints, to avoid any possibility of leaks. They were fixed to the cabin floor with Jubilee clips and snaked along behind the rear crew seats (where they were a damned nuisance) until they dived down to the outside air through a pair of redundant flare tubes. From here they were led forward, attached to the aircraft's skin by more jubilee clips and fed into the rear keel fuel tanks. It was all very crude but it worked.

Close up of the aerials above and below the tailplane of a Nimrod. These counteracted the stability lost by the addition of a refuelling probe.

The fitting of the probe to the forward fuselage was bad for the already marginal directional stability of the aircraft. To balance this a wooden fillet was fitted under the tail, enclosing the tail bumper. To add a little more stability, aerials, already fitted to the Nimrod R.1, were fixed above and below each tailplane. They were not connected to any radio equipment and must have caused some puzzles for Argentinean Intelligence. These modifications seemed visually to be inadequate. However, again, they worked. I should add that when the Falklands war was over the system was redesigned to make it a tidy, fully approved design.

In parallel with the flight refuelling trials we had to check that the modifications had not affected the handling characteristics of the aircraft. On the 29th of April, Al McDicken and I carried out stalling and VMCA tests. On the 30th of April, Johnny and Tony carried out the first wet contacts in XV232 and on the 1st of May the service was given the release for

XV232 carried out the first 'wet' contacts with the new probe.

daylight use and XV238, the first Nimrod fitted with the AAR system, was delivered to RAF Kinloss. On the 2nd of May, Johnny and I carried out the first night contacts and the night release was issued the next day. These and other clearances were issued by a senior civil servant who lived with us for the duration. I am afraid that I do not remember his name, a great shame, as he was superb, never flinching from taking a decision. The release signals were sent on my telex machine as soon as the debriefing was over and he and I had agreed that the aircraft was up to standard. This was often after midnight. It was hard but exciting work and extended the aircraft's range to some 12,000 miles, which allowed the Task Force to proceed on it's way to the islands.

The first real operational flight for a Nimrod was by an aircraft of 201 Squadron on the 12th of May. The sortie was due to last 15 hours; involve two prods (refuellings) and the support of six Victor tankers. It was on this flight that an Argentinean Navy Boeing 707 was sighted. This aircraft had been shadowing the fleet for several days and it's attentions were extremely unwelcome. However the Nimrod carried no weapons with which it could fire on the 707 so it was allowed on it's way unmolested. This was clearly unacceptable so the telephone in John Scott-Wilson's office rang yet again.

"How long would it take to fit and test Sidewinder missiles to the Nimrod?"

"Two weeks."

"Okay, go ahead."

Argentinean Boeing 707s posed a threat to the fleet, that is until the Nimrod became a fighter.

The Nimrod had originally been designed to carry two SS.12 air to surface missiles under it's wings. These had never gone into service so the requirement was deleted but the wiring was still in situ, as were the wing reinforcement points. BAe Warton quickly designed the necessary pods and on the 26th of May Tony Banfield and I flew 229 down to Boscombe Down where it was fitted with a pair of Sidewinders on each pod and we carried out a rapid series of tests to prove the handling qualities. On the morning of the 27th of May we flew to try out the acquisition mode of the missiles. This we did by flying up behind an unsuspecting civil aircraft and getting the characteristic growl in my headset that denoted that the missile had acquired it's target; a noise I had never heard before, indeed I had never fired or carried a missile before in my life. With this aspect proved to our satisfaction, we landed and the ground crew made the missiles live. We were now ready for the live firing. At the briefing it was made plain that this was to be a Company trial observed by the Boscombe Down pilot Tony Banfield. Tony was disappointed; he wanted the honour of being the first to fire a missile from the Nimrod. I compromised; I said that I would carry out the attack on the Jindivik drone target but that he could press the firing button. Not a big decision as the button on his side was the only one connected.

The Jindivik was an unmanned target drone.

We took off and flew north until we reached Ailsa Craig the small island between the Mull of Kintyre and Girvan on the West Coast of the mainland of Scotland. On the way I sneaked up behind a passing Victor tanker and tried out the acquisition growl. It worked. It was a beautiful day and we could see all the way to the Welsh coast from our 10,000-foot height. We began to circle the island, talking to RAE Aberporth who controlled the missile range that stretched to the south of us. They warned us that they were about to launch our target and read off the ranges to us as the little unmanned aircraft flew steadily south. I circled the aircraft tightly with all of the crew who could looking out to the north. After an anxious age, Tony spotted it and I told Aberporth that we had it in sight, I swung our four-engined "fighter" in behind the drone and Aberporth sent the signal to ignite the flare being towed behind the Jindvik. This flare was necessary as the Sidewinder is a heat-seeking missile. We swiftly caught up with our target and as I heard the growl I told Tony to fire. To our utter surprise we were engulfed in a dense cloud of smoke and a deafening roar as the missile sped away. None of us had ever fired a missile before. As the Sidewinder neared it's prey with it's characteristic snake like motion, the smoke cleared and we had a perfect view of the missile striking the flare. Complete success, and so home for tea.

The sequel to our efforts was interesting. A few days after the flight Woodford was visited by a party of foreign guests. As they walked from the 748 that had brought them they happened to pass a Nimrod fully armed with four Sidewinders. A photograph was taken of the party, which appeared in the press the next day. In it one could clearly see the missiles. The Argentinean 707 was never seen again.

Whilst I was engaged in the Sidewinder tests Al McDicken was busy carrying out similar tests on the Harpoon air-to-surface anti-ship missile. These were carried internally in the Nimrod's weapon bay and therefore had to fall clear before the rocket motor could be ignited. The carriage trials were quickly completed and the arrangements made for a live firing. Such was the speed of things Al was never told that there was a ten-second gap between pressing the button and the missile falling away. Thus they entered the firing range and the rear crew made the necessary preparations, taking some little time. Al, getting anxious about the approaching range boundary, kept asking how they were doing and only got the okay as they reached the limit. He pressed the button, called missile gone and waited, and waited. As they left the range area and Al was about to call a misfire there was a roar and the missile sped away skimming the surface of the sea. An anxious time passed until they were sure that the Harpoon had run out of fuel and fallen harmlessly into the sea. Another success.

Referred to on many occasions as 'the world's largest fighter', photographs of the Nimrod actually carrying the Sidewinders are rare. The rails can be clearly seen under the wings of XV234.

During August of 1982, the RAF began to prepare for the long-term protection of the Falklands. They knew that now the Islands had been re-taken the Nimrod force would need to land at Port Stanley airport. The runway at Stanley was very short and they needed advice on how to somehow shorten the aircraft's landing run. We were asked to carry out feasibility trials and I gave the task to Tony Hawkes, giving him a free hand to do what he felt necessary. After a few days he told me that he had a solution to the problem.

He proposed that the landing be carried out with airbrakes extended and full reverse thrust being selected just before touch down; a technique that we had used successfully many times on the 748. This would ensure that the aircraft touched down at the desired spot and with immediate full reverse, thus cutting out the variations that always come with different pilot techniques. He carried out stalls with the airbrakes out as a preliminary to actual landing and found no problem. He then carried out several airbrakes out landings and again found no difficulty. He did a dozen or so landings using his recommended full reverse in the flare technique and found it very easy. He invited me to come with him and try it for myself. This I did on the 26th of August at RAE Bedford. We did this again over the next two days to refine the technique and then recommended it to the RAF. Now that peace was declared the service reverted to it's usual cautious self and refused to have anything to do with what they considered a radical departure from the norm. Crews might be tempted to land like that all the time and the powers that be, without trying it out, said that this would produce heavy landings. No matter what I said the service would not listen and went ahead and landed at Stanley using the normal landing technique and thus, in my opinion, risking overruns. Luckily, the skill of the crews prevented this.

A Hercules C.1K trails it's refuelling drogue.

The Falklands conflict made great demands on the tanker force. As I have already said a typical Nimrod sortie required six Victor tankers and attacks such as the 'Black Buck' Vulcan raid needed even more. The whole of the Victor force was in Ascension and was being augmented by C-130 Hercules that had been converted to the tanker role by Marshals of Cambridge. Marshals had done a superb job in a very short time but the Hercules was only suitable as a tanker for the slower aircraft. Of course back at home the RAF still had to fulfil it's NATO commitments, which required tankers to support the Tornado squadrons. The VC.10 tankers had yet to enter service and there was no way to bring this forward. However, the Hose Drum Units, (HDUs), for the VC.10's were in store awaiting fitment and were thus available for use. What the Air Force did have was a surplus of Vulcans that were due to be phased out in 1983. The famous telephone went again and we were asked if it was feasible to make these aircraft into tankers. Another crash programme on top of that of the Nimrod was instituted. This one would take two and a half months.

The first phase of the programme was to survey a Vulcan to see what areas of the airframe we could use to house the HDU. Luckily, as already explained, we had a static Vulcan of our own at Woodford, this enabled us to carry out a thorough survey and it was concluded that the ECM bulge on the fuselage tail was just large enough to house an HDU. This bulge was empty as the ECM gear that used to be in it had been superceded by smaller equipment fitted elsewhere, but the wiring for power supplies for the equipment was still in place. It would be necessary to pipe fuel to the HDU but this was relatively simple, using the already standard bomb bay overload tank as a collector tank for the whole fuel system. The main difficulty was to

An HDU is lifted into place on a Vulcan K.2. The whole unit was encased in the 'Council Skip'.

design and fit a housing for the drogue. The drogue on the end of the hose is the receptacle into which the pilot of the receiver aircraft pushes his probe to obtain his fuel. This needs to be housed in the tanker aircraft in such a way as to control the airflow around it to let the drogue be blown out of the housing when required. Once clear of the housing, the airflow would continue to drag the hose out against a brake to control the speed of it's extension. There was also a need to provide traffic lights to signal to the receiver when he is clear to prod and when he must withdraw. I am sorry to have to explain the procedure in such sexy terms but the truth is that it is all rather sexy.

Alan Clegg, our Chief Designer Military, was given the task of designing the housing and quickly sketched an inelegant piece of kit that immediately became known as the 'Council Skip'. Alan was a charming but forceful Northern man who bullied and pushed all around him. He was ideal for the task. His council skip was made of angle iron and sheet aluminium. It had a moveable flap at the front to control the airflow and the traffic lights, red, amber and green, were positioned either side of the rear aperture. The size of the throat in the skip was critical and was arrived at empirically by carving large blocks of Styrofoam into suitable shapes and sticking them to the sides by double-sided tape. After each test flight these blocks would be modified, often with Alan's penknife, and we would try again. I have an abiding memory of Alan in the middle of the night taking his ties off, measuring the throat with it and then running round the hangar calling for a tape measure to check the size.

I had not flown a Vulcan since 1963 and then only two or three times at Boscombe Down. We were lucky to have Al McDicken and Harry Nelson on the staff who were both ex-Vulcan Captains. However I was determined not to miss this chance of renewing my acquaintanceship with this great aircraft. On May the 17th, I flew the company Pup to RAF Waddington and underwent Vulcan simulator training, just four hours in the

XH560 was one of six Vulcans converted into tankers.

box and lucky to get it. I had to wait until June the 15th before I was allowed to get my hands on an aircraft when Harry Nelson and I collected Vulcan B.2 XH560 from Waddington and flew it to Woodford for modification. On the 18th June Al, and I flew XH561 on the first flight of a Vulcan tanker.

The flight was not completely successful as we had a power control failure due to my finger trouble, and Al had to land it with only partial control. He did this with great skill and we only suffered a scrape of the skip that was soon repaired. The aircraft was turned round and after repairs we flew it again that afternoon. On June the 22nd I sat beside Johnny Cruse in Nimrod XV229 as he carried out the first flight-refuelling sortie against a Vulcan tanker. It was a complete success. It was agreed by all that the Vulcan made a superb tanker. The airflow behind it was smooth and the hose completely steady. On the 13th of July I flew 229 with Wg Cdr Ian Strachan, the boss of B Squadron Boscombe Down and an old student of mine, as he assessed the Vulcan's suitability for service as a tanker. The first sortie was by day and we flew again to assess the night suitability some time near midnight on the same day. The aircraft passed with flying colours.

The markings under the Vulcan and the night lighting threw up some interesting aspects. I was asked to suggest what was necessary to provide markings to guide the receiver pilots. All tankers have such markings that indicate to a pilot when he is lined up with the drogue and to show the correct angle of approach. I quickly sketched how this could be done; a straight red line outlined in white ran up the centre of the skip and continued along the rear of the aircraft's fuselage, and this provided line up. Another similar line was drawn across the skip and when the receiver was approaching at the correct angle this line joined up with two similar lines, one on each wing trailing edge. This all proved to be excellent in practice but the design process had it's ridiculous side. Passers-by were highly amused by the sight of a group of middle aged men in their business suits lying on the ground under the aircraft arguing about the correct placement of the lines. Night lighting involved a similar scenario. Floodlights were set into either side of the skip and these illuminated a white painted area under the trailing edge of each wing. It was necessary to see how effective this was on the ground before we involved a receiver aircraft in an airborne trial. One must remember that all this was being done in high summer and it was only truly dark after midnight. Also the lighting on the surrounding roads lit up the sky and made true blackness impossible. A telephone call was made to the local council and wartime necessity was quoted to ask them to turn off the streetlights in the district. They co-operated readily and so the same group of middle-aged men was seen to be lying under the aircraft again as the floodlights and traffic lights were tried out and adjusted. The verdict of the RAF pilots who eventually flew behind the Vulcan tanker was that the markings and the lighting were the best of all the tankers.

The Falklands effort at Woodford was over by September 1982. It had been quite an experience and, dare I say it, very enjoyable. For many of our servicemen in the islands it had of course been anything but enjoyable but we had enjoyed feeling that we were involved and doing our bit to support them. The feeling at Woodford was tremendous. It was truly the wartime spirit. It was marvellous to see the production line full again with Vulcans. Throughout the period everybody gave 100%, men were working so long that they had to be told to go home and rest, and it wasn't just for the overtime money. I must also pay tribute to the unions for their flexibility and patriotism. There was never a problem about rates for the job or working hours. I am sure that if someone had approached a shop steward with a complaint they would have been told to get on with it. The whole affair showed that the right spirit was not dead in Britain. It was there all the time, just below the surface and I am sure that it still is. Serendipity played a big part in the affair. Johnny Cruse was experienced in flight refuelling from his Vulcan/Olympus testing days at Filton, Al McDicken and Harry Nelson were both ex-Vulcan captains and I had been on a Valiant tanker squadron. Luckily we all had good memories, as our experience was long past.

Vulcan K.2 XH560 refuels Vulcan B.2 XL426 over the North Sea in 1983. XL426 survives at Southend Airport with the civil registration G-VJET. (Harry Holmes)

Chapter Nine

The Advanced Turbo-Prop

I had been in the Chief Test Pilot's seat for a whole week in February 1981 when Ken Edgerton, the Chief Salesman, rang me and said,

"Robby, as you know we are thinking about making a new aircraft, the Advanced Turbo-prop. What we need is something to make it really advanced to fit the name. Any thoughts?"

I had heard rumours about the new aircraft, it was to be a development of the 748, bigger and with new engines, but I had not yet been involved in any discussions on the new project. I thought for a moment,

"Well, Ken the latest thing around is the glass cockpit, you know the pilot's instruments being displayed on cathode ray tubes. That should be a start."

From such an inauspicious beginning was to grow a fascinating project that was to give me my chance for a first flight, a thing that few test pilots have the privilege to do these days.

The pace of the preliminary design process increased by the day. My first action was to insist that the Flight Operations department be involved at every stage. To this end I appointed a Project Pilot and a deputy. For Project Pilot I needed someone with experience but who would not be afraid to be adventurous to think laterally. Tony Hawkes was the obvious choice. His early test flying had been on fighter aircraft such as the Harrier so he was not a dyed in the wool transport man. He could be charming, touchy and argumentative but I thought this to be a plus. In the event we had very few disputes and much of the design of the ATP is down to him. As his deputy I chose Harry Nelson, a man of great energy who would be a good replacement if something happened to Tony. I never had cause to regret either of my choices.

Alan Troughton had been appointed as Chief Designer and his brief was for minimum change from the 748 except of course to increase the seating capacity from 48 to 70. These two requirements were to some extent incompatible and were the cause of many disputes between the local Manchester Divisional Board and the main BAe Directors. It is a little known fact that the most difficult sale of a new aircraft is to the Main Board. This was made even harder because many members of the Board were keen to get rid of the civil side of BAe, to concentrate on the military side and to merely manufacture components for Airbus. Of course they have now managed to do just that but in the eighties we were embarrassing them by continuing to make a profit. They merely made life hard for us by scrutinising our every move and holding regular project reviews that required all involved to waste a lot of time preparing for them. All very necessary I dare say but very frustrating and a process that almost guarantees under-investment in a project.

The main responsibilities of the test pilots in the design stage of any project are the design of the flight deck and the quality of control. For this we needed a flight deck mock up and some sort of simulator. We eventually got the former but it was part of the complete fuselage mock up and was primarily a sales tool. This became a problem quite soon. For the simulator we made use of the Hatfield variable stability simulator. This was very useful but it had to be shared and therefore we had to book it in advance so were unable to put new control characteristics on it at short notice. It also meant that Tony and I spent a lot of time driving up and down the M1. We were able to make rapid progress on the flight deck layout, all the time constrained by the fact that it's dimensions were basically that of the 748. However, in 1984 the sales force was relocated to Stevenage and, against what I saw as logic, they took the mock up with them and set it up at Hatfield. In theory we still had access to it but in practice we were now unable to just pop across the airfield to check whether a new item of equipment could be properly seen, reached and operated. We managed to stagger by however and produced a quite acceptable flight deck layout.

The main change on the flight deck was the glass cockpit, or as we learnt to call it the EFIS, (Electronic Flight Instrument System). EFIS was quite new in civil aircraft, although it was starting to be put in bigger aircraft such as the Boeing 757 and the Airbus 320. I sampled all these and they were wonderful but these aircraft were completely new designs and space had been designed into the flight deck to accommodate the large cathode ray tubes (CRTs). We had no such luxury. We looked at some small EFIS's that were coming onto the market but these were designed for General Aviation (GA) that is corporate aircraft and other puddle jumpers. We needed one suitable for an airliner flying the airways on a daily basis. It was decided to put the matter out for tender.

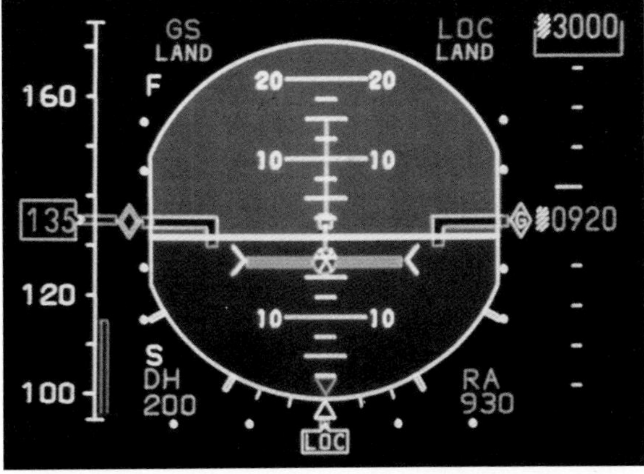

Typical example of the futuristic instrument display in the cockpit of the ATP.

Several companies responded but most submissions were developments of their GA equipment; Smiths put forward a completely new proposal that they were prepared to develop jointly with BAe. I favoured this for several reasons. We had a good rapport with Smiths having used their instruments and autopilots in many of our past aircraft. Also the ability to influence the design was very attractive. However, as far as I was concerned the deciding factor was that they were quite close, in Cheltenham, and we could drive down to see them at short notice. Another big plus was that Smiths could put their prototype equipment into the Advanced Flight Deck at BAe Weybridge for us to play with. This facility had been in use for many years having been made for a national study of future flight decks. This study was now largely moribund but the flight deck, which was a fixed base simulator, was still available for BAe programmes. Another big advantage was that John Wilson was working on it and was available to give us his advice. John had been a test pilot at Hatfield; he had in fact been John Cunningham's co-pilot on the first flight of the Comet. He had stopped flying but had made the study of flight decks his special province and was to prove invaluable to us.

The choice of engines for our new aeroplane was not simple. The 748 series 2 was fitted with the good old, reliable Rolls Royce Dart turboprop engines of 2,105 shp, a wonderful engine but not powerful enough for the ATP and rather fuel thirsty. Even the larger version in the RAF Andover C.1 of 2,970 shp whilst being powerful enough was too heavy and not sufficiently economic. We would dearly loved to have chosen a British engine but Rolls had put all its money into large jet engines and had stopped all development of turbo-props, we would therefore have to look elsewhere. We put the requirement out to tender and the best bid by far came from the Canadian arm of Pratt and Whitney with their PW124 of 2,570 shp. Now we had to choose propellers to put on the engines. One of our design aims was to match the extremely quiet HS.146 for noise, to do this we needed slow turning propellers, which meant big ones to produce the required thrust. The other variable was the number of blades per engine. A study narrowed the choice down to six blades and BAe joined with Hamilton Standard to produce an airscrew of 13ft 9in diameter. At some juncture I was asked how much ground clearance we needed. As we had had some trouble with the 748 sustaining propeller damage on rough strips I said that the ATP's clearance should be no worse than that of the 748. A good reply I thought. I did not know that the designers would achieve this clearance by increasing the length of the nose gear leg. I was present with Charles Masefield when the aircraft was lowered off its jacks for the very first time and we saw with dismay that it had a really ugly nose up/tail down attitude. This was hastily corrected on the second aircraft but I was blamed of course.

The PW124 was a very modern engine and had a FADEC, a Full Authority Digital Control System that protected it from damage. This required information such as altitude, airspeed and stage of flight, take off, cruise etc. As the design of the aircraft progressed other items of equipment also required digital information and the most economic way of providing this was by a digital bus bar, an information channel that carried all the necessary information from which the various bits of kit chose what they wanted. This, plus other factors, dictated that the CAA would not allow us to certificate the ATP as a modified 748 but only as a totally new type. A critical decision as it meant that we could not rely on "granny rights" from the 748 but would have to meet the latest European JARs, (Joint Airworthiness Requirements). The most difficult of these to meet was the secondary control system. Under the new requirements if the control cables or rods were severed for any reason there had to be a secondary system that would allow the pilot to retain sufficient control to get the aircraft home safely. The cause of the severance was assumed to be an explosion in the engine that expelled large chunks of the turbine or compressor discs. These would penetrate the fuselage and cut the control runs. The size of the chunks was specified, as was the width of the swathe that they cut. The most obvious way of avoiding this was to armour the vulnerable area of the fuselage. This was not allowed as the chunks were assumed to have infinite mass and would penetrate anything. The logical conclusion was that they would also cut through the other engine, although this was ignored. The 748 control cables were set in a neat straight line under the cabin floor and ideally positioned to all be cut at the same time. This caused hours of worry.

A special design meeting was called, chaired by Alan Troughton, to discuss the secondary control system. It was a large meeting including such design gurus as Pete Teagle and Bill Stableford. The problem was described to me, as this was the first time that I had heard of the new requirement. As we were not allowed to armour the fuselage the next obvious solution was to provide another set of control cables in the cabin roof where they would be clear of the assumed destructive swathe. This would however increase the all up weight, which was already critical, also it would increase the control friction and produce handling problems. I listened for some time and then timidly asked where the autopilot control motors were to be positioned, were they under the flight deck floor or were they at the control surfaces?

"At the control surfaces," said Alan. Could we, I asked, somehow use them to control the aircraft after a control cut? Could we connect the pilot's controls to them and let him fly the aircraft by a form of "Fly by wire"? The meeting went silent for a moment and then everybody began to talk at once.

"Okay," said Alan, "Let's run with that. Bill, see if it's feasible"

The first idea that Bill came up with was for the autopilot to cut in and take control as soon as a control cut was detected. I discussed this with Nick Warner, CAA's Chief Test Pilot, but he felt that the subsequent landing would prove to be difficult. Bill then evolved a way of using only the inner circuits of the autopilot, the amplifiers, to provide signals to the actuators from the pilot's controls. This system would be automatically switched on when a control cable went slack after a break. This promised well but there was a history of the tension in control cable loops after a single cable break imposing a force on the control surface and thereby creating an uncontrollable situation. Bill solved this by ensuring that, when the tension was lost in one side of the cable loop, the tensioner in the pulley collapsed, thus making the single break into a double break that imposed no force on the control surface.

Another new requirement was for the aircraft to be controllable after a jammed control circuit. Again, Bill solved the problem. He realised that the secondary control system could be used to provide a channel of control for one aileron or elevator when the other jammed if we gave the pilot a means of separating the control surfaces. A device that separated the surfaces when a force over a certain amount was applied to the pilot's control wheel was designed to do this. A mechanical lever was also provided as a back up. Thus, after a jam either the left hand pilot retained control through the normal control runs or the right hand pilot had control through the secondary "fly by wire" system.

You may have gathered that I consider Bill Stapleford to be some kind of a genius. He and I and Tony Hawkes worked closely together for many months, all the time consulting the CAA to check that they were happy with the principal of our radical system. We checked the likely handling qualities of the secondary system on the Hatfield design simulator in a series of tests until we were all happy that they were acceptable. The acid test would of course be testing it in the air on the actual aircraft. It was disappointing to me that I would never be able to try it out as the system would not be on the first two aircraft and I would have retired before it was ready to be tested.

Overleaf: This is the mock-up ATP flight deck and shows the EFIS to good effect. The aileron disconnect control is at the bottom of the picture next to the aileron trim wheel.

In 1988 the secondary control system was tested and proved to be just as good as we had predicted. I hope of course that it is never used in anger.

Whilst I was primarily responsible for the pilot's side of the secondary control system, Tony worked with John Wilson and Smiths on the EFIS. They jointly came up with an excellent layout with the primary instruments, the artificial horizon, airspeed indicator, vertical speed indicator, radar altimeter and pressure altimeter on the small upper CRT and the compass rose on the lower. The pressure altimeter presentation that they evolved was, I thought, brilliant. It is well known that the human brain is very good at detecting changes of a needle on a circular dial but not very good at doing the same on a digital readout. You get the same effect with a digital watch, it is very accurate but it requires actually reading the figures to tell the time. Time on an old-fashioned dial watch is instinctively read by the position of the hands. John and Tony showed me their solution that, I thought, gave the best of both worlds. It had a digital read out in the centre of a dial that had a small marker rotating round it that showed any movement from level, the marker being at the top at every thousand feet. It worked beautifully and we had a succession of airline pilots fly it on the simulator, even Nick Warner of the CAA agreed that it worked. However, the CAA was in the middle of a dispute with Airbus over their proposal to put a digital altimeter on their EFIS and could not bring themselves to agree with our proposal and thereby weaken their argument. We therefore had to delete our ingenious instrument and put an old-fashioned dial altimeter beside the EFIS. Of course, Airbus eventually won the argument but too late for us to take advantage of their small victory.

In 1984, Charles Masefield, who was by now Managing Director at Woodford, recognised that the project was stalling a little. It was somewhat openended and needed a shot in the arm. He therefore announced that the aircraft's maiden flight would take place on the 6th of August 1986. It was unprecedented that such an announcement should be made two years in advance. There was a lot of muttering in the design and production departments but Charles' charisma overrode any objections and the very precise date concentrated our minds and gave a lot of power to the elbow of Mike Taylor, the Project Manager, who now drove the proceedings forward with increased pace. It would be shaming to us all if we failed to meet the deadline. Later the actual time of take off became set at 10 AM, to allow for our guests to take coffee whilst the aircraft was airborne and to wander out to witness the first landing before sitting down to lunch. Public relations rule, OK? Actually the date was very logical. We agreed that it would be silly to fly the aircraft in 1986 and not get it to the Farnborough show. We estimated how long we would require to carry out all the preliminary tests to satisfy the CAA that it was a safe aircraft to display at the show, which began on the 28th of August; three weeks was the answer, with no room for errors. Thus the 6th was arrived at as the latest time for the first flight.

The aircraft was rolled out from New Assembly early in 1986 and was towed over to the Flight Sheds where the final preparations would be made. Unlike many roll outs there was no ceremony. This had been reserved for the first flight. For some totally absurd reason we had changed our advertising agency from Arthur Gibson, the well-known air-to-air photographer, to an agency that had no knowledge or sympathy for aviation. I had just one meeting with them in the presence of Richard Fletcher, the new Managing Director, and BAe's chief PR man. The two representatives of the agency were young and rather trendy. They opened with their concept of the arrangements for the great day.

"I see it," said the senior man, "With the aircraft starting up and taxiing out of the hangar through a cloud of smoke lit by lasers and to the music of the Squadronnaires band."

"We can't do that," I said, "There is far too much to do before we fly. We have to do things methodically and anyway it isn't safe to taxy out of a hangar, we need to be towed."

"Let me finish." He said.

"You already have." I replied standing up and leaving the room.

"But we have already hired the band." He called after me plaintively.

Our own head PR man, Harry Holmes, told me later that he quite agreed with me.

The ATP Prototype G-MAPT being towed across Woodford in early 1986 without ceremony.

The sales people told us proudly that they had arranged with CAA for the aircraft to have a special registration. They showed us a drawing of the colour scheme, which was the usual BAe scheme of a white fuselage with orange, red and blue cheat lines sweeping up into broader lines across the tail. On the fin was the registration that they had chosen, intended to spell out "GO ATP". It read G-OATP; all of us immediately said "Goat Pee!" The salesmen took away their drawing and re-registered the aircraft G-MATP, however, an ATP of Manx Airlines eventually did get Goat Pee.

The ground testing of the aircraft accelerated as the time for the first flight approached. Tony, Harry and I spent many hours doing the engine runs that not only fine tuned the engine systems but gave us much-needed familiarisation of handling the engines. The runs went mostly without a hitch but we did have one drama. We were doing full power runs a few days before the maiden flight. The parameters of the engine systems were being controlled by a Hewlett-Packard computer down the back. With the port engine still at full power, the engineer in charge of the tests inputted the parameters for the next test. To my horror the engine torque rose at an alarming rate into the red zone. I instinctively slammed the power lever closed and shut the engine down. The tests were cancelled and the Pratt and Whitney rep ordered an over-torque check. As soon as possible we examined the recordings and found much to our relief that I had prevented the torque from going over the absolute design limit. The over-torque check confirmed that the engine was not harmed so we were still on schedule, we had no spare.

The 13ft 9in airscrews warranted a slight nose up attitude, this was later modified on the production aircraft.

The aircraft first turned it's wheels under it's own power two days before the fateful day. I released the brakes and increased the power by means of the auxiliary ground control roll over levers. We moved forward to the waves of the few spectators and I tried the brakes and the nose wheel steering. I turned right onto the taxy way and down the short runway, turning right again onto the main runway. The weather was fine with a 10-knot wind straight down runway 25, ideal. I allowed the aircraft to accelerate to a moderate speed as we backtracked to the end of the runway where I turned to point into wind. The engines were exercised and I set full power against the brakes. We waited until the required torque was indicated and recorded and when everyone was satisfied I released the brakes. The aircraft accelerated slowly at first and then briskly. When we were about halfway down the runway and at some 70 knots, I closed the power levers and waited for the expected rapid deceleration from the disking of the propellers. It did not happen, the aircraft continued towards the end of the runway at high speed. I tried the roll over levers that should bring in the reverse pitch but they did not function. The only thing left was to stand on the brakes, which I did. We stopped quite close to the runway's end with very hot brakes and taxied back to the Flight Sheds. It was found to be a software glitch that was solved in a couple of hours so we were able to repeat the runs later in the evening. All was well and after shut down I handed the aircraft back to the technicians to prepare for the great day.

Jetstream 200 G-BHYM was the chase aircraft for the first flight of the ATP. It seems hard to believe that 'YM' is today, an exhibit in the RAF Museum at Cosford. (Harry Holmes)

We had consulted with all departments over several weeks and had evolved a flight test plan for the first flight. Of course every design department wanted a piece of the action to give them some reassurance that their bit functioned properly. We could not do all that was wanted but we reached a fair compromise that covered the initial flight envelope and the final document was approved by the Chief Designer, the Head of Flight Test and myself. The Flight Crew was to be myself as Captain, Tony Hawkes as co-pilot and Barry Lomas as the Flight Test Engineer. Barry was an old hand at this sort of thing and I could think of nobody better to be on the instrumentation panel in the cabin and run the test programme.

Overleaf: The ATP on it's first flight on the 6th August 1986.

G-MATP

SH AEROSPACE
ATP

The day before the flight we held the main briefing. It was crowded; I had never seen the room so full. I was to chair the meeting and as I walked in only my chair was vacant. I sat down and looked around; everyone was silent and the atmosphere was rather tense, after all none of us had ever been in this situation before.

"Something special on?" I said, in attempt to lighten the mood. I was partly successful and we settled down to do a line-by-line analysis of the flight.

After take-off we would be joined by the Jetstream chase aircraft flown by Peter Henley, my deputy. He would observe the undercarriage retraction and then formate on us to give us a quick check on the accuracy of our airspeed indicators and altimeters. We would then separate and the ATP would depart for the airspace over Lincolnshire where we would complete the rest of the programme before rendezvousing with Arthur Gibson's small aircraft and one of our own 748s for air-to-air photography. Then we would head for home. In all a flight of about three hours if all went well. If it didn't we would be home much sooner.

I felt that all the people in my department would wish to be involved in what was an historic event (the ATP would probably be the last civil airliner to be designed and produced wholly in the UK) I therefore allotted a task to each of the members. Some would be flying in the chase and photographic aircraft; others would be busy on the ground. For instance, Kevin Moorehouse would be in the control tower to cover any help that we might need in the event of difficulty. He would be heading a team composed of one person from each of the design departments. They were there to give us advice on any technical problems, which Kevin would pass on to us over the radio.

I hoped that their help would not be needed. We would, when we could, give the team regular updates on the progress of the tests on a discrete frequency but most of the time we would be out of contact listening to Eastern Radar who would be warning us of conflicting traffic, a constant problem in test flying. Harry Holmes had arranged another radio task for us. Halfway through the flight I was to make a broadcast which would be linked into the Public Address system in the hospitality tent on the airfield. I doubted that any of our guests would hear it over the clink of glasses.

One of the last tasks of the day for me was to sign a mass of first day covers that we would carry the next day and which would be sold for charity. With that over I went down into the hangar to have a short time to myself with the aircraft. Most of the ground crew had gone home so I was able to become a little maudlin in private. I walked round G-MATP and stroked it's flanks, admiring what I still think is a good looking aeroplane. I climbed onto the flight deck, sat in my seat and mentally rehearsed the take-off actions. I knew them by heart of course but it never hurts to practise and anyway this was the first time that I had really been alone in the beast. Eventually, I tore myself away and went home to my pillar of normality, my dear wife Tricia. She would be in the audience tomorrow, driven there by my son Simon. I had not been able to get any tickets for my daughter Keri and her husband Bill but they would be watching from outside the airfield boundary.

The big day dawned cold, rainy and with a gusty wind. Sod's law, as we had been enjoying good weather over the last week or two. I drove in to work early, dropping into the hangar to see that everything was all right, and then going to my office to clear up any outstanding administrative matters. Sue my secretary was already there and wished me luck. I looked out of the window where the first of the aircraft bringing our visitors were taxying in.

The final briefing was at 08:30 hrs and was a small affair compared to yesterday's mammoth affair. This was just a run through the test plan to ensure that all involved were certain of their parts. Eric Gladwin, the SATCO, confirmed that Manchester Airport would give us some priority for takeoff and I read out the latest Met forecast. There was to be no change, the rain would continue although the cloud base would be quite rea-sonable, 2-3000 feet. The worst aspect was that the wind would be straight across the runway at up to 20 knots. Ah well, met forecasts were usually wrong and things could change before we landed. With the briefing over we all went our separate ways, I returned to my office and stood looking out at a pan that had filled up during my absence. The ATP now stood off to the right and was sur-rounded by visitors and photographers. There were television cameras and vans on the edge of the pan and the left-hand side was now full of vis-iting aircraft. It was a busy scene, the ATP provid-ing the only bright spot in the drizzle blowing

across the pan. As I stood taking this all in and feeling a little apprehensive about the spotlight that I was about to step into, Richard Fletcher, the MD, came in and stood beside me. He too looked at the scrum below where the Chairman of BAe had now arrived.

"I just came to wish you luck Robby," he said, "The weather looks a bit iffy. Just remember it's your decision. If you say your not flying, that's fine."

I imagined the fuss and disappointment if I did indeed say no go. I chickened out,

"No, Richard, it's okay. We will fly."

At 09:15 hrs the three of us walked out of the calm of the department into the media circus outside. The crowd parted like the Red Sea although I did not feel like Moses, not unless he led the Jews into exile wearing a dazzling orange flying suit such as the PR men had provided us with. We were forced to pause on the aircraft steps for photographs until I tired of the flashing strobes and led my men into the cabin. The steps were pulled away and Barry closed the door. At last we were in the environment that we understood and it was peaceful. We strapped into our parachutes and seat harnesses and began the checks. It is worth saying at this point that one of the drawbacks to testing large air-craft is that there are no ejection seats. Our sole escape aid was a knotted rope that stretched from the flight deck to the overwing escape hatches, from which we would have to bail out in the event of a nasty. I did not fancy our chances of doing this in a spin or similar emergency. The knotted rope had been the cause of much gallows humour over the last few days.

The checklist had been assembled by ourselves over the past few months and was as untried as the aircraft but it seemed to work. One by one the engines were started and after Barry had recorded control deflections and reported that he was ready I called for taxy.

"Avro One request taxy"

"Avro One you are clear to taxy to the holding point of runway 25", Linda replied. The crowd had by now cleared to the sidelines and I advanced the roll over levers and we began to move. The adventure began.

ATP over the Lincolnshire coast during it's faultless maiden flight.

I taxyed the ATP slowly as we had plenty of time to make our 10:00 hrs take off. We trundled down the short runway and were cleared to enter and backtrack to the take off point on runway 25. As we passed the hospitality marquee on our right I could see the crowd in front of it cowering under their umbrellas. They would be glad when we had left and they could retreat to the shelter of the tent. I could not see Tricia or Simon but, knowing my dear realistic wife, she would already have been inside. We reached the end of the runway and I turned the aircraft to face down it. Five minutes to go, just right. We carried out the over-speed governor checks on the engines, set the flaps to 22 degrees and the trims to neutral and called for take off.

"Avro One you are cleared for take off. The wind is 160 13 knots. After take off turn left onto a heading of 100 and climb to 4,000 feet squawking 4561."

Holding the aircraft on the foot brakes I advanced the roll over levers to maximum and then began to push the main power levers to the take off torque. We would be spot on the 10:00 hrs take-off time. As the power levers reached the forward position the central warning red light started to flash and the warning horn sounded. We quickly tried to identify the cause and I called the technical group in the tower for help. Very little was forthcoming. We narrowed it down to a configuration warning switch so Tony and I checked all the possible reasons and then looked at each other and shrugged, I cancelled the warning. A mis-set micro-switch; a common fault. I released the brakes and we began the take off run. We were five minutes late, not bad for a departure time set two years ago. At 85 knots I raised the nose and the aircraft unstuck, it was in its element for the first time. I turned left onto the required heading and called for 15 degrees of flap and climb power. Peter Henley in the Jetstream reported that he was in position on our starboard side and I asked Tony to raise the undercarriage. Peter reported that it looked good and we cleaned up and began the climb. I gently tried all the controls and invited Tony to do the same. We both thought them good, the only thing less than perfect was the change of directional trim with power. Something that was to remain with us for all time.

We changed frequency to Midland Radar and were cleared to Flight Level 85 (8,500 feet). Peter, who had been with us all the way, now closed in to close formation and we compared speed indications to check our uncalibrated instruments against his. They compared within a knot. We descended to FL60 and compared speeds as we went down. They were exactly the same. Midlands now directed us to our rendezvous with our 748 camera aircraft, flown by Harry Nelson and with Arthur Gibson's Cessna. We spent 10 minutes posing for publicity pictures before peeling away to complete the PE (position error) checks against the Jetstream. Flutter checks at 200 knots came next where we performed control jerks in both directions on all three controls. These were merely preliminary checks to prove the recording system. The real flutter checks would come a lot later in the development programme. We then performed a full suite of stalls down to the stick shaker and checked that the speeds were as forecast. We climbed to FL200 where we repeated the flutter checks. This seemed a good time to make the promised broadcast to the audience waiting in the marquee.

Harry Holmes, the one PR man in whom I had perfect trust, had asked me to make this broadcast if I had time. It was to be patched into the PA system but only announced at the last minute. I had given what I would say some thought and had decided that a little humour would lighten the mood. I had no wish to appear to be like the steely eyed test pilots in "Sound Barrier".

"Good morning everybody. Things are going very well. We have absolutely no problems. You can tell the designer chappie that he has a winner here." Of course the last sentence comes from the Tony Hancock test pilot sketch. It seemed appropriate at the time but was destined to dog me for years. Not everybody remembered Hancock's Half-Hour.

'Avro One' arriving safe and sound at Woodford, despite a 23 knot crosswind.

Nevertheless, although I was mocking the seriousness of the occasion, the phrase was true.

The next twenty minutes were occupied with more flutter checks and a level cruise to check that we could achieve our design speeds. It was now 12:25 hrs and we had completed the full test plan so I called for recovery to base and Midlands Radar handed us over to Woodford. We planned to make an ILS approach to test the new EFIS so ATC vectored us for a straight in approach. The new instruments were a revelation, clear and easy to interpret. Our problem came when the tower passed us the actual weather. It was still drizzling and the surface wind was 170 degrees 23 knots, pretty close to our desired demonstrated crosswind limit. It would be unique to establish this limit on a first flight also a southerly wind at Woodford always meant a bumpy ride due to turbulence off Alderley Edge. We broke cloud at 2,000 feet into a murky day and as promised it was very bumpy. I flew the aircraft on the ILS Glide Slope down to 300 feet and treated the audience to a close view of the aircraft by flying past the crowd. This also allowed everyone to judge how quiet the ATP was; in fact Peter Teagle, one of the designers, asked a nearby tractor driver to turn his engine off so that he could hear our engines. Mind you, the strong wind was blowing the noise away from them. I turned downwind where I lowered the undercarriage and Peter in the Jetstream reported that all appeared good. I turned onto finals and called for full flap, setting up a fairly long approach at 100 to 105 knots. The crosswind now became obvious, to hold the centre line it was necessary to point the nose 15 degrees to the left and I viewed the runway through the extreme right hand side of my windscreen. We came over the threshold and I held the drift as I cut the power and raised the nose. Just before touch down I pushed the right

Robby during one of many interviews immediately after the flight.

rudder to cancel the drift and applied nearly full left aileron to hold that wing down. We touched down smoothly and I retarded the roll over levers to give a small amount of reverse thrust and allowed the aircraft to slow down to walking pace. It was over; we had been in the air for 2 hours and 45 minutes and had achieved all our objectives. We had done it and we felt very good. The aircraft had given no problems and promised to fulfil all it's design expectations. We taxied past the audience and could see them applauding. Now we were going to be thrust back into the media spotlight and be exposed to the press conference. A necessary evil I supposed.

The ATP flight crew on the 6th August 1986; Barry Lomas (Left), Robby Robinson (centre) and Tony Hawkes (right).

We parked in the spot from which we had departed and looked down on the media scrum. I could see the chairman waiting at the foot of the steps surrounded by photographers. We unstrapped and stood up just inside the closed door and shook each other's hands. I combed my hair and, taking a deep breath, opened the door. I led my crew down the steps and grasped Sir Austin Pearce's proffered hand.

"Congratulations, a tricky wind wasn't it?" I agreed and introduced Tony and Barry. We were then surrounded by the press photographers and resigned ourselves to their ministrations until Richard Fletcher rescued us and pushed us into a waiting car, which whisked us off to the hospitality tent. We entered the tent rather like astronauts back from the moon, which felt rather ridiculous for the first flight of a medium sized airliner. I knew that publicity was necessary for the sake of sales but we all thought that this was a bit over the top. However, if you can't beat them join them. I was met by Tricia who kissed me and asked how it went.

"It went fine, see you later." I had no chance to say more as we were ushered onto the platform where we were exposed to questions from the various air correspondents, including Geoff Cooper of the Daily Telegraph, who used to be my boss in the Ministry of Defence some years before. The only thing that I can remember saying was a nugget that I had been saving. I read out my horoscope from the Daily Mail of the previous day,

"If using new equipment read the instructions carefully." Good advice except that there were no instructions. At last we were released and sat down to partake of a splendid lunch, imbibing a little too freely perhaps and staying rather too long, which earned us a mild reproof when we eventually arrived at the debriefing where the designers had been waiting with increasing impatience. Still, I could say with truth that the aircraft had behaved perfectly.

That evening there was a dance in the tent with music from the Squadronnaires who you will remember had already been hired before I refused to go along with the PR people. Tricia and I took the floor, which was quite rare, and a good time was had by all. I said to Tony that we should take turns to fly the rest of the test programme and that he and Harry Nelson should fly tomorrow's tests. This he did and, as he flew as my co-pilot when I was Captain, he flew on all the flights up to and including the Farnborough show. This was quite a strain on him as we had to complete 30 hours flying over twelve flights to show the CAA that the aircraft was safe to display there. This we did and three weeks from the first flight we flew to Farnborough to demonstrate to the Flight Committee that our display obeyed the rules.

The Flight Committee controls the display at the show and is responsible for the safety of the proceedings. It is composed of all the UK Chief Test Pilots and, at the time, was chaired by the Commanding Officer of RAE Farnborough. I had been a member of this elite committee since 1982 but even so I had to pass the appraisal procedure. The Chairman that year was Group Captain David Scouller who I had shared a desk with at ETPS in 1962; the test flying fraternity is a small one. Every morning before flying commences the Chairman holds a briefing for the participating pilots. This takes place in an old bell tent and is a friendly affair. A famous past chairman is Reggie Spiers who, after viewing a spirited display in a Bulldog trainer by John Blair, the Scottish Aviation CTP, said:

"John, dear boy, could you take two turns off the bottom of your spin and put them on the top?"

John took the point.

The show week went well for us and the ATP raised a lot of interest. It was visited by many potential buyers and VIPs whilst in the Static Park, including the Duke of Edinburgh. For this visit Tony and I were called to be in attendance, I would stand at the bottom of the steps and Tony was to sit in the cockpit and tell the Duke about the aircraft. We were duly in our places at the correct time and I could see the Duke and his entourage moving down the line towards us. Just as he approached us I was roughly jostled aside by a group of Chinese who climbed the steps and crowded onto the flight deck. I tried to explain to them that a VIP was expected but was swept aside as they did not appear to speak English. Prince Phillip arrived and I had to explain that the cockpit had been taken over by a crowd of Chinamen. "Good," he said, "We are going there next month, I must meet them."

At that moment the Chinese party came down the steps and the Duke stepped forward to greet them. Their leader stared at him and said abruptly, "Who you with?" The Duke with a twinkle in his eye replied, "Oh haven't you met Robby Robinson the Chief Test Pilot?" and left me to deal with them as he went into the aircraft where he spent a considerable time questioning Tony about it's performance.

We flew everyday with no unserviceabilities, which is pretty good for a brand new aircraft. It intrigued watchers as we used reverse thrust to back into our parking slot after each display. I have in my log book a parking ticket issued by the Ministry of Defence Police which warns me that I had contravened the Establishment Regulations namely:

    1. Reversing without the use of wing mirrors.

    2. Failing to observe traffic signs.

    3. Parking on triple yellow lines.

    4. Having no certificate of airworthiness.

I think he was joking.

It was a busy week as we not only flew the display routines but carried out several test flights and a formation photo call. We also flew with Raymond Baxter on board to record a commentary for television. On the 8th of September, we took the aircraft to Hatfield to demonstrate it to the Chinese CAAC, who incidentally offered me a job as their CTP when I retired! Later that day we flew home for a well earned short rest. Now the real work began.

An ATP in British Midland markings performs a surface water test.

Our aim was to get the ATP into airline service by the end of September 1987. I was due to retire at the compulsory age of 55 in March 1987 but not only would this have been a pity but we needed all hands to the pumps so Charles Masefield asked me to stay on for an extra six months. I needed no urging. To get into full airline service we would have to not only complete all the requirements laid down by the CAA but a period of line trials flown by our first customer, British Midlands Airways. This would be the acid test, as it is well known in the testing business that no matter how much the aircraft is flown by test pilots, the average airline pilot will find areas of weakness of which the designers had not thought. Some of these things are simple; such as where do the pilots put their wet coats and hats? It sounds silly but I found out how important these things are when flying for Air Bridge later on. BMA's Chief Pilot John Bowker flew with us a lot and helped to iron out many of these details, I wish that he could have been with us from the start. A lesson for any future projects.

Tony, Harry, our other pilots and myself flew many hours over the next months. Of course we not only had to fly the ATP but fly the production tests of the last 748s coming off the line and the Nimrod MR2 and AEW trials. The most exacting flying from the pilot's point of view were the flutter tests. These consisted of diving the aircraft to achieve the desired speed and, at the required height, sharply rapping the control wheel to the left, the right, forwards and backwards. The rudders are similarly tested by being kicked left and right. The object of these tests is to ensure that the control surfaces do not "flutter" that is cause the wings or fuselage to flex and vibrate, perhaps to destruction. The nerve-racking bit is that if they do flutter there is little that you can do about it. One puts one's trust in the engineer's calculations. The higher the speed required the less time that one has to complete the tests before passing through the allowable height band. To do the tests at the designed maximum speed the aircraft has to be climbed to it's maximum height and dived with full power. You are lucky if you manage to complete just the aileron tests in one dive so many hours are spent on the exercise with repeated climbs and dives.

The last test flights I carried out were the smoke tests and the icing trials. Every aircraft has to be capable of clearing smoke from the flight deck within a minute of the pilots carrying out the required drill. To prove this Tony and I, on two flights, were sealed into the flight deck with the help of plasticine around the edges of the door. Thick stage smoke was then fed in, with us wearing goggles and smoke masks and with the autopilot in, until we could not see the instruments in front of us. The engineers in the back then called time and we took the prescribed emergency actions. We called as soon as we could read the instruments. It was all very unnatural. For the initial icing trials we had to fly longitudinal stability tests with shaped blocks of polystyrene fitted to the leading edges of the wings to simulate ice being picked up in flight. Not a difficult test but no aircraft would ever take off in this condition so we raised the unstick speed and crossed our fingers. There were no problems.

The CAA pilot Jock Reid and his constant companion Keith Perrin, the Flight Test Engineer, flew with us several times to see how things were going until they finally issued a restricted Certificate of Airworthiness that enabled BMA to carry out the in service trials. Unfortunately my extension as CTP was up at the end of November 1987 so I was not around to see the final results and the aircraft's full C of A being issued. However the trials went well and the aircraft entered full service on time. I meanwhile, had to look to my own future.

Overleaf: The team at Farnborough in 1986. On the far right, in flying suits, are Carol Elliot, Flight Test Observer, Tony Hawkes and the author. Under the 'A' of ATP on the steps, is Billy McGeehan, who was in charge of the ground crew.

BRITISH AEROSPACE
ATP
G-MATP

At the age of 55 I felt too young to retire, in any case I needed to supplement my rather moderate pension. There were no jobs available within the company that took my fancy so I decided to leave and try my luck in the airline industry. I answered several advertisements and was offered two or three posts but accepted the offer of an immediate Captaincy with Air Bridge at East Midlands airport flying the Merchantman, a freighter version of the Vanguard. I spent a happy four and a half years with that delightful company flying freight by night around Europe, enjoying the feeling of being an indian again and not a chief. We operated rather like tramp steamers, taking all types of freight from newspapers to horses and including eels from Lough Neagh and car components from Bilbao. I most enjoyed the racehorse runs from Dublin to France when I could go back to the freight bay and chat to the beautiful beasts. Our routes spanned a wide variety of airfields in Europe and we spent happy weekends in places like Dublin and Amsterdam. All this had to come to an end as I neared the age of sixty and I was resigned to full retirement when fate stepped in again.

A Vickers Merchantman o Air Bridge based at Eas Midlands airport ir Leicestershire.

The airline very generously lent me G-APEJ Merchantman to fly a display at the Woodford Air show on the 22nd of June 1991. I flew my standard routine and happily wheeled around the circuit in the large turboprop. In the considerable crowd was my old friend Charles Masefield who wrote to me thanking me for my efforts and offering me a job at Woodford to teach on the ATP simulator when I finished at Air Bridge. I had another six months to go with the airline but Air Bridge was reducing the number of Merchantmen on the fleet and needed fewer pilots so I volunteered to go, allowing them to retain a young First Officer at the start of his career.

I settled into the job of simulator instructor and, despite the terrible hours, enjoyed the sometimes onerous task of converting pilots of many nations onto the aircraft for which I had largely been responsible. Later the production of the BAe 146 and it's simulator were moved from Hatfield, which closed, to Woodford and I doubled on that as well as the later 146RJ simulator. The company in another seemingly illogical act moved the ATP simulator and production line to Prestwick. This was to try and get Taiwan to buy the whole 146 project, including Woodford, by hiving off anything that did not belong to the

BAe 146 is another success story to come from the British Aviation industry. It was in production from 1983 to 2001 becoming another victim of the slump in world air travel as a result of 9/11.

project so as to show a neat package. Of course the sale fell through and the money spent on the relocation wasted. The move meant that I lost contact with the ATP, which I regretted. I felt very proud and privileged to have been associated with such a successful proj-

ect and watched with interest it's progress in airline service over the following years. Sadly, although it still remains in service with several airlines and is well thought of for it's incredible fuel efficiency, it became the victim of corporate politics and production ceased in the mid-nineties. At that time BAe was trying to reduce development costs by merging with the French company Aérospatiale. This company produced the ATR 72, which was a direct competitor for the ATP. Only one of these aircraft could survive so, in the usual self-destructive British way, the ATP was cancelled. The really ironic thing was that the merger was unsuccessful and the companies separated. It was of course too late to reinstate the ATP production line.

The ATR 72 was the direct competition to the ATP, sadly an amalgamation with Aérospatiale saw the French aircraft come out on top.

During this period I re-joined the RAF as a Flying Officer in the Voluntary Reserve to fly Chipmunks at RAF Woodvale, north of Liverpool. The CO of the Air Experience Flight was Martin Mayer, an old friend and colleague who had been the CO of ETPS a few years after me. Once a week I would drive to Woodvale and spend the day flying ATC cadets around the area to hopefully encourage them to join the RAF. Many of them flew the aircraft very well, often the girls better than the boys, and it was pleasing whenever one of them became enthusiastic about aviation. I learnt that Liverpool girls never say yes or no. If you asked them whether they wanted me to do some aerobatics they would say "Go on then" or "You're all right". I loved the Chipmunk, a real lady, but in 1996 we changed to the Bulldog, which I did not like. At this time I failed my medical due to high blood pressure, so I regretfully resigned my second Commission and stopped flying for good, I thought, and concentrated on my simulator instructing.

In 1997, at the Society of Experimental Test Pilots' symposium, Georgio Clementi, the Managing Director of the International Test Pilot School, approached me to become the school's Director of Flight Test. The school had just moved to Woodford so it was too good

an offer to miss. I had to renew my Pilot's Licence as I had let it lapse. This meant taking a medical with my old friend Ronnie Rheisler. Luckily I had by now managed to lower my blood pressure with medication and he passed me. I also had to take the CAA ground examination for an aircraft type, as I had not flown a civil registered aircraft for over five years. I chose the ATP as I thought that I knew something about it. I called in a few favours and was given a free ground school and simulator course at Prestwick and a flying test on the ATP

'A real lady', the Chipmunk will be around for many years to come since it's mass arrival on the civilian market in the mid-nineties.

at Warton. I passed it all, even the flying test, which I was a little apprehensive about as I had flown nothing that big for six years. In July I began what I thought was my last job as I was by now over sixty-five. Within weeks of me taking over a great tragedy occurred. Benoit Niclause, the school's French Chief Test Pilot and a Spanish student crashed on a test flight and both were killed. Beverly, Georgio's wife, and I had the terrible duty of telling Benoit's wife Ann, a task that I never thought that I would have to perform again.

I faced the usual barrage of media attention as well as that of the Air Accident Investigation Branch. We eventually came out the other side of the problem and I took over as Chief Test Pilot as well as Director of Flight Test.

Over the next two and a half years I taught the esoteric art of test flying to a succession of pilots and engineers from a wide-ranging selection of countries. There were Canadians, Swedes, Germans, Indonesians, Spaniards, Italians, Singaporeans and Australians. It was an interesting time and I was always impressed with the high quality of the students that the various services and companies sent us. It also enabled me to try many more aircraft types, always an attractive thing for a test pilot. In 1999 BAE Systems, as BAe had now become, decided that they had to get rid of all lodger units on the airfield so the school moved to Coventry Airport. I was not prepared to commute each day as Tricia had by now been diagnosed with cancer, so I resigned and prepared for full retirement. Fate stepped in again and I was asked to come back to teach on the 146 and RJ simulators again. This work dried up after the terrible events of September 11th 2001 in New York. So at the age of sixty-nine I took early retirement but I am still open to offers.

Just one more snapshot. As a result of the ATP project the Guild of Air Pilots and Navigators (GAPAN) awarded me the Derry and Richard's Medal. The presentation was to be at the Mansion House in London and King Hussein of Jordan would be presenting the awards. Tricia and I booked into the Royal Garden Hotel in Kensington and we changed into our finery in good time before taking a taxi to the venue. This was the first time I had worn white tie and tails and I felt an idiot until we mingled with the other guests who all wore the same uniform, at least the men did. We sat down to dinner in the magnificent banqueting hall and it was a grand occasion although I have no memory of the actual food served; I was probably too excited. Eventually the awards ceremony began. As each name was announced the recipient had to walk round the perimeter of the room to reach the King who, of course, sat in the centre of the top table. At last my turn came and I rose from my place, walked briskly away from the top table to the rear of the room where I would begin my long walk around the room to the King. As I stepped off the carpet onto the highly polished wood floor behind a row of pillars my feet slipped and I performed one of those prat falls you see in the pantomime, landing flat on my back with all the wind knocked out of me. I hastily picked myself up and looked round to see if it had been noticed. Everyone was still looking at the King, but the King was looking at me. I completed my circuit and arrived beside His Majesty who grinned at me and said in his deep brown voice,

"Ah! Mr. Robinson. Did you have a good trip?"

The answer is yes; I have had a very good trip. Fifty years of undetected crime.

A&AEE	*Aeroplane & Armament Experimental Establishment*
AAR	*Air to Air Refuelling*
ADF	*Airborne Direction Finder*
AEW	*Airborne Early Warning*
ATC	*Air Traffic Control*
ATP	*Advanced Turbo Prop*
ATPL	*Air Transport Pilots License*
AWACS	*Airborne Warning and Control System*
BA	*British Airways*
BAe	*British Aerospace*
BMA	*British Midland Airways*
C of A	*Certificate of Airworthiness*
CAA	*Civil Aviation Authority*
CAAC	*China's old state airline*
CO	*Commanding Officer*
CRT	*Cathode Ray Tube*
CTP	*Chief Test Pilot*
DC-10	*Douglas Commercial*
DERA	*Defense Evaluation Research Agency*
DME	*Distance Measuring Equipment*
ECM	*Electronic Counters Measures*
EFIS	*Electronic Flight Instrument System*
ETPS	*Empire Test Pilots School*
FADEC	*Full Authority Digital Control System*
GA	*General Aviation*
GAPAN	*Guild of Air Pilots and Navigators*
HDU	*Hose Drum Unit*
HF	*High Frequency*
ILS	*Instrument Landing System*
JAR	*Joint Airworthiness Requirements*
MD	*Managing Director*
MoD	*Ministry of Defence*
MR	*Maritime Reconnaissance*
NDB	*Non Directional Beacon*
PR	*Public Relations*
RAE	*Royal Aircraft Establisment*
R & R	*Rest & Recreation*
RPM	*Revolutions per Minute*
RR	*Rolls Royce*
S of F	*Superintendent of Flying*
SATCO	*Senior Air Traffic Control Officer*
SBAC	*Society of British Aerospace Companies*
Shp	*Shaft Horse Power*
TGT	*Turbine Gas Temps*
TP	*Test Pilot*
TTAS	*The Trinidad and Tobago Air Services*
UDI	*The Unilateral Declaration of Independence*
VG	*Vortex Generator*
VHF	*Very High Frequency*
VIP	*Very Important Person*
WVS	*Womens Voluntary Service*